*from the*

# Father's Heart

## Growth & Healing

### DAILY DEVOTIONAL

*Tailored for Life's Seasons -
Emotionally & Spiritually*

# MARIA KEAR

From the Father's Heart (Book 2)
*Growth & Healing - Daily Devotional*
*Tailored for Life's Seasons —*
*Emotionally and Spiritually.*

Copyright © 2024 by Maria Kear
All rights reserved, including the right of
reproduction in whole or in part in any form.

First Edition March 2025

STM Press
    978-1-966240-02-0 (paperback)
    978-1-966240-03-7 (ebook)

*All scripture references are from the New
Living Translation unless otherwise noted.*

*All word definitions were taken from the
Strong's Online Concordance unless
otherwise noted.*

Designed by Suzanne Parrott
Cover Image created using Midjourney

**From the
Father's Heart
series**

*Rest & Reflection*
*Growth & Healing*
*Joy & Adventure*
*Hope & Possibilities*

# Acknowledgements

I want to thank my 5 family – Jeff, Matthew, Katherine and Abigail (I'm the 5th) for always cheering me on when I have crazy ideas like writing my own books. Even if they think I'm weird, they still love me.

I want to thank Debra Rothrock and Angie Davidson for their eyes on the text when they had a moment to make sure my grammar and punctuation were in line.

I want to thank Suzanne Fyhrie Parrott for being my publishing partner and the one who made all the details come together so my voice could be heard in the earth.

# Dedication

This book is dedicated to the current and future Jesus lovers who will never tire of reading God's Words or of hearing Him speak. To the ones who love and seek out adventure with Holy Spirit as guide and partner. To the ones who are not satisfied with only what this world offers, but long for news from their place of origin – Heaven. And to those brave enough to hug their Bibles to their chests with wide smiles and tear-stained faces. You have found your people!

# Author's Note

The first book I learned to read was the King James Version of the Holy Bible. I was five years old when I picked up the book and just started reading. My mom told me that no one taught me to read, but that I just started reading one day.

When I asked her how that was possible, she replied that from the moment I came home from the hospital to live with her and my grandparents Wheeler in Meggett, SC, my granddaddy Wheeler read to me, making sure I could see each page and picture as he read. We believe that his gift of reading to me from day one prepared my brain to be an early and life-long lover of books, especially the Bible.

Thank you, Granddaddy Wheeler.

# Day 92

## First Things First

Deuteronomy 21-22 / Luke 9:51-10:12 / Psalm 74 / Proverbs 12:11

Did you know there is a cost to following Jesus? Some think we simply decide to follow Him and then our life goes on. Some realize that without the drawing of God's Spirit, we could not even say "yes" to Jesus Christ. Once we belong to the family of God, what is required of us? And yes, I realize what follows could be a lengthy answer and that I'll barely scratch the surface.

What does the Lord require?

Micah 6:8 says this, "No, O people, the Lord has told you what is good, and this is what he requires of you: to do what is right, to love mercy, and to walk humbly with your God."

In Luke 9:57-62 there were two people addressed. The first wanted to follow Jesus, and the second was asked by Jesus to follow Him. Neither of these ended up following Jesus because the one who wanted to follow Him had not counted the cost. He told Jesus that he needed to go bury his father, taking care of the family business. The one who Jesus asked to follow wanted to say goodbye to his family first.

Both reasons for not following were good and loving, with honorable desires to care for their families. However, Jesus knew that once each of these men returned to his family, he would be entangled again with the "cares of the world" and would not return to follow Him.

I am not saying we should not care for our families—of course we should—but we must not place this concern above our love, devotion, and relationship with Christ. And I believe that is the point.

Did you know that our families can become idols? Anything that is placed above Jesus in our affections is an idol. In placing Jesus first, we will still love and care for our families. We are blessed to keep both Jesus and our families as priorities when each is placed in the proper order.

Let's examine the passage in Micah again. God requires three things: to do what is right, to love mercy, and to walk humbly with our God. Let's dig a little deeper to better understand these so we can apply them to our lives.

> The definition of "to do what is right" is "do no unrighteousness in judgment, for judgment is God's."

> We show that we "love mercy" when we have "zeal, love and kindness (offered toward anyone.)"

> To "walk humbly" is defined this way, "be humble, submissive and modest (before God who is greater.)"

As you can see, our relationship with God and others is most important. Love God; love others. We've talked before about the fact that we cannot say we love God if we do not love others.

Perhaps the two people in Luke who wanted to follow Jesus did not yet realize their need for Him, or perhaps they were not yet ready to make Him the top priority. No one knows what they were thinking (except Jesus – and that's why He responded as He did. He always sees the hearts of men and women.), but their actions tell the story.

What do your actions show about your willingness to follow Jesus? If He asks, do you follow? Or do you have caveats that must first be met? Remember that if we seek first the Kingdom of God, all things will be added to us. Meaning, when we say "yes" to Jesus, the things that are precious to us will be taken care of as well!

# Day 93

## *Though the Earth is Shaking*

Deuteronomy 23-25 / Luke 10:13-37 / Psalm 75 / Proverbs 12:12-14

"When the earth quakes and its people live in turmoil, I am the one who keeps its foundations firm. Interlude." —Psalm 75:3

During the season of Easter, as we remember the death, burial, and resurrection of Jesus, there is great hope. I'm sure His followers during that time were discouraged and afraid. They didn't know He was going to be crucified, and I'm sure they wondered what was going to happen after His death.

We have an advantage because we know how the story ends. At the end of Jesus's encounter with death, His Father brought Him back to life. In His death and resurrection, He gifted us with eternal life. Jesus's agony brought us peace with God and the expectation of one day seeing Him face to face.

So, even as our world is being shaken, and even though we can't see what's ahead, we must look to the One who holds everything together with His powerful word. He's not shaken or surprised. Why would He be? He marched straight into Hell and took the keys of death, Hell, and the grave away from the enemy who used to roar. I say, "Used to roar," because Jesus took all his power away that day.

I'm sure you sense that God is up to something big. He will not leave His people feeling alone and afraid. He will not allow us to be overwhelmed. Yes, we will still feel the rumbles, but we do not have to be shaken.

As you sense things being shifted, remember that your foundation in the Lord remains firm. In Him, you will be made strong. So, keep your eyes set on His face and allow your heart to be held in His hands. Determine that you will speak only in faith and keep pressing forward. You are not alone. God is with you!

# Day 94

## *Expectations in Prayer*

Deuteronomy 26-27 / Luke 10:38-11:13 / Psalm 76 / Proverbs 12:15-17

Once again today, we are reading in the Gospels about prayer. Both John and Jesus taught their disciples to pray. I don't know that John's teaching on prayer is recorded; at least, I couldn't find it. But Jesus's teaching is recorded in varying forms in the Gospels.

Everyone is familiar with The Lord's Prayer. In today's reading of Luke, I appreciate how Jesus followed the prayer with a story, along with some practical instructions for those listening.

Jesus told the story of two friends, one in need of bread and one who was reluctant to get out of bed to help the first. As the first friend persisted, the sleeping friend finally got up to help him. There is an example in the story that leads us to understand we must continue to ask, seek and knock. We must continue to be persistent when we need something, both physically and in prayer.

Then Jesus said, "For everyone who asks, receives. Everyone who seeks, finds. And to everyone who knocks, the door will be opened."
—Luke 11:10

Jesus reminded those listening that if their own children asked for certain things, they would not give them something harmful. Jesus knows we love our children and would not purposefully hurt them. He also knows that His Father knows what His children need, and He would not give us something harmful.

"So if you sinful people know how to give good gifts to your children, how much more will your Heavenly Father give the Holy Spirit to those who ask Him."
—Luke 11:13

When we're asking for something in prayer, we don't usually see clearly what is needed. We may think we know what we want and what would be best, but God has a bird's-eye view. He sees our lives from beginning to end, and He knows what will best help us navigate through life.

Some become disheartened or even angry when their prayers appear not to be answered. But verse 10 says that if we ask, we receive. How do these two thoughts align?

Our perspective on what we need is often not the same as God's perspective. We may think we need a certain thing. However, God knows that things will either not be helpful or will derail us in some way. So, He answers, but when it's not according to our expectations, we assume He did not answer.

It will be interesting to get to Heaven one day, where we'll see the "map of our lives." Then we'll know why life seemed difficult or confusing at times. We'll understand why God seemed to be slow to answer or not to have answered at all. And we'll smile, thank Him, and praise Him for His perfect will.

He loves us so much! So, today, if you're not sure how to pray, ask for the Holy Spirit, and according to verse 13, you will receive that gift. And with the gift of the Holy Spirit, you'll receive wisdom, boldness, patience, and maybe even the thing you most long for, that specific answer to your prayer.

# Day 95

## Be Filled with Light

Deuteronomy 28 / Luke 10:11:14-36 / Psalm 77 / Proverbs 12:18

"No one lights a lamp and then hides it or puts it under a basket. Instead, a lamp is placed on a stand, where its light can be seen by all who enter the house. Your eye is like a lamp that provides light for your body. When your eye is healthy, your whole body is filled with light. But when it is unhealthy, your body is filled with darkness. Make sure that the light you think you have is not actually darkness. If you are filled with light, with no dark corners, then your whole life will be radiant, as though a floodlight were filling you with light."—Luke 11:33-36

Let's talk about these verses because I feel they are foundational to our Christian walk. To me, this passage speaks about the partnership between truth and proper discernment.

If your eye is a lamp for your body, your eye must be clear so that light, or truth, can enter your understanding. The eye may refer to our worldview, which is based either on God's truth or some skewed beliefs we've adopted throughout our lives. I say that boldly, because only God's truth is infallible and able to stand all tests.

Lately, the Lord has been speaking to me about having proper doctrine and interpreting scripture from that understanding. In some circles, for example, legalism skews the truth of scripture. God is teaching me to view scripture through the lens of love, grace, and redemption.

He's also teaching me it is not my job to judge the way others follow Him but to judge my own walk and my own grasp of truth. I wonder what other kinds of things might cloud our eyes. Anger, judgment, unforgiveness, and many other things are likely suspects.

Imagine that you have a big picture window in your home, and it's the beginning of spring with all the trees and flowers blooming outside. The bad news is your picture window is covered with mud and dirt from a recent hurricane and you can't see anything clearly.

Not only can you not see the view, but you're also disgusted by the nasty, streaked dirt all over your beautiful window. It will probably take you a good hour or two to scrape, clean and put final touches to that window so you can see the beautiful view. It will, however, be worth the effort for the rewards you'll gain.

What might it look like to clear the view of our eyes? I think it would involve repentance, forgiveness, and taking a proper inventory of our own hearts. We would have to remove the "log from our own eye before removing the speck from our friend's eye." (Matthew 7:5)

This is what I'm choosing to do. I'm choosing to focus on my own heart and my own beliefs and whether they align with scripture. After that, I hope to be able to take time to help, support and love my brothers and sisters. After I've removed that log from my eye, maybe I can help others remove the splinter from theirs.

# Day 96

*You Have a Choice to Make*

Deuteronomy 29-30 / Luke 11:37-12:7
Psalm 78:1-31 / Proverbs 12:19-20

"Today I have given you the choice between life and death, between blessings and curses. Now I call on Heaven and earth to witness the choice you make. Oh, that you would choose life, so that you and your descendants might live! You can make this choice by loving the Lord your God, obeying him, and committing yourself firmly to him. This is the key to your life. And if you love and obey the Lord, you will live long in the land the Lord swore to give your ancestors Abraham, Isaac, and Jacob." —Deuteronomy 30:19-20

Just like God said in the Old Testament, He still gives us a choice between life and death, between blessings and curses. This is another wide topic that we won't have time to fully investigate, but it's worth beginning to explore.

We cannot love, obey, or commit ourselves to God if we have not first been regenerated or born again. The Father has provided the path to regeneration through the sacrifice of His Son.

We are in the time of year when we celebrate Resurrection Day—a day that marks Christianity as unique from all other religions. Our God is alive. The other "gods" are dead.

Once we're established into the family of God through faith in Jesus Christ, we still have many choices every day for the rest of our lives. Will we ask God for His help in life's situations, or will we slug it out for ourselves? We can choose.

We may come up with some really good ideas as we consider what to do in each situation, but if we ask God, He has the best way for us to respond.

I was talking to my youngest daughter recently about how exciting it is to follow Christ. Those who are not yet made alive in Christ don't understand that. They may think Christianity is boring or restrictive, but I've found that following Jesus is filled with mystery and adventure!

Suppose you have a decision you're facing and you're not sure what is the best choice. You weigh your options. You might even make a pros and cons list; however, that list may be very inconclusive. You may ask for the opinions of others who have made similar choices to find out what they did. However, you may finish this exercise of fact-finding and still not know what to do.

What if we instead asked God for wisdom and direction, even before we made a list or asked anyone else for advice? I've mentioned this many times in my writing, and talk about it often with friends. God has a path laid out for us that is full of adventure, blessings, life, mystery, and surprises.

God sees both the rocks and the smooth places ahead. He can help us navigate both. The bonus for us is that we are learning two things: to keep our eyes on Him and to give Him glory for every part we experience. We can even give Him glory in the rocky places. Why? Because these are the places where we learn the most.

As we continue through our lives, we grow and mature. We also learn to better depend on God, and our character is shaped to be more like Jesus. Once we come through the rocky times, we usually have a better appreciation for the smooth places.

In considering the many choices within the realm of life and blessings (because no one would intentionally choose death and curses!), seek God first. Ask Him for His opinion and input. I think it's a good idea to start your day by asking Him to lead you, and then check in at different points during the day. Not only will you find yourself walking a full and beautiful life, but you'll also find that your relationship with God is thriving. Because that is the point of all this interaction: to find out Who God is and become more like Him.

Happy Choosing!

# Day 97

## *He Wants to Give Us Everything*

Deuteronomy 31:1-32:27 / Luke 12:8-34
Psalm 78:32-55 / Proverbs 12:21-23

"Yes, a person is a fool to store up earthly wealth
but not have a rich relationship with God."
—Luke 12:21

"Seek the Kingdom of God above all else, and He will
give you everything you need. So don't be afraid, little flock.
For it gives your Father great happiness to
give you the Kingdom."
—Luke 12:31-32

As I read the scriptures for today, my heart warmed. I sensed God's great love for His people. He provided for and loved them, even knowing they would betray Him by worshiping idols. And He still does the same for us.

Not only did I sense His great love, but I also sensed a deep grief and disappointment that they, and we, were going to stray in their love for Him. Jesus died for the sake of His relationship with us, but also for our relationships with each other. I know He places a high priority on connection and community.

Imagine loving someone to the point of giving one of your children to die so you could have a relationship with them, and then they turn around and wander away to give themselves to a lifestyle that will destroy them. Can you feel the pain of that? I can.

God sent His Son to die and be resurrected so that we might have eternal life, knowing that we would not be faithful. He sent His Son, knowing that some would reject Him while others would receive Him. From my human perspective, I would want a guarantee that my offering would be received before I'd want to give it. But that's not how God's Kingdom works!

May I ask you a question? Do you give only when you think what you have will be received well? Do you give because you'll be thanked? Do you give in hopes of gaining favor with others?

We cannot give with these expectations. We must give because God tells us to, and with no thought of the outcome. We cannot control the responses of others. We can only control our obedience to His voice.

And that's what Jesus did. He obeyed His Father even though He would be rejected. This is no "sissy pants" Gospel! This life with Christ is not for the faint of heart. We must be brave to follow Christ and to obey Him. Are we willing?

If we are, our Father is excited to give us all the good things of His Kingdom. Would you rather have earthly wealth or Heavenly treasure? You may be wondering how we acquire Heavenly treasure. We receive His rewards by obeying Him and impacting the lives of others. The process is simple, but it will cost all you have.

Are you ready to follow Him? Are you one who will say, "Yes!" when God asks?

# Day 98

## *The Life of a Leader*

Deuteronomy 32:28-52 / Luke 12:35-59
Psalm 78:56-64 / Proverbs 12:24

"Be dressed for service and keep your lamps burning."
—Luke 12:25

"A faithful, sensible servant is one to whom the master
can give the responsibility of managing his other household
servants and feeding them."
—Luke 12:42

"Work hard and become a leader." —Proverbs 12:24a

As I read the above verses, I noticed a theme of what it looks like to become a faithful servant and follower of Jesus Christ. All of us can be faithful and obey God as we walk along the path He designed for us. But how many of us find that path, much less actively walk on it according to His purpose?

My love of mystery and adventure keeps me watching for His purposes and listening for His call. I've always been the one, at least as far back as I can remember, who wanted to "go out with a blaze of glory." Meaning I want to get to Heaven knowing I found what God intended for me to do and that I did those things with my whole heart.

I don't want to live a partial or half-life; I want to live a full, abundant life. If I know there's a plan and a path, it is my desire to find that plan and path and follow both with everything in me.

Sure, I'll make mistakes. But if my desire is to please and obey God, I believe I'm more than halfway there, and I believe He'll help make sure I find those hidden gems He planned for me.

This, to me, is what it looks like to be a leader. A leader only leads well when they are following Him for themselves first. Once others see that we know where we are going, they are inclined to follow our example. Not to follow in our path but to follow in finding their own path.

I believe the first part of my calling is to follow Christ. The second part is for you to follow me as I follow Christ. This does not mean you follow me; it means you follow my example and find Jesus Christ for yourself.

What does your path look like? Or what do you imagine it looks like? At one point, I imagined my path looked like a dirt path with stones here and there. But I don't think that's at all what it looks like!

Let's imagine it together. If God is good and the Creator of the universe, I know my path is filled with colors, sights, and sounds that would be so unimaginably beautiful. There is greenery, beautiful flowers, singing birds, and gently flowing brooks.

Here's what I see in my spirit considering God's goodness. I see a wide area to walk that has no visible boundaries. The boundaries are there, but the path is a broad place as spoken of in Psalm 18:19 in The Passion Translation.

"His love broke open the way, and
He brought me into a beautiful, broad place."

Yes, there are times when the path narrows, and the walk is hard. Sometimes I struggle to walk uphill, and sometimes I'm thankful for the rest of going down the next hill. I think there is beauty as far as the eye can see.

I also know there are dark places where I can see only my feet and a small circle of light around them as it says in Psalm 119:105.

"Your Word is a lamp to my feet and a light to my path."

Some areas are bright and joyful, and some are dark and difficult. But there is one thing that does not change; Jesus Christ is always with me. He never leaves me. Sometimes His voice will be loud, and sometimes a whisper. Sometimes I'll laugh and sometimes I'll cry. Sometimes I'll run and sometimes I'll rest.

I know I'm only scratching the surface of what God has planned with my description. I'm also confident that "no eye has seen, no ear has heard, and no mind has imagined what God has prepared for those who love Him." (1 Corinthians 2:9 NLT)

I will end this entry by saying to you, "Be dressed. Be ready. Keep walking. Find adventure. Love God and love others."

# Day 99

## Good Things Come in Small Packages

Deuteronomy 33 / Luke 13:1-21 / Psalm 78:65-72 / Proverbs 12:25

The Parable of the Mustard Seed from Luke 13:18-19.

"Then Jesus said, 'What is the Kingdom of God like?
How can I illustrate it? It is like a tiny mustard seed that
a man planted in a garden; it grows and becomes a tree,
and the birds make nests in its branches.'"

The Parable of the Yeast from Luke 13:20-21.

He also asked, "What else is the Kingdom of God like?
It is like the yeast a woman used in making bread.
Even though she put only a little yeast in three measures
of flour, it permeated every part of the dough."

I love these two parables that Jesus told. The coming of the Kingdom of God, along with the Messiah coming to earth, was expected to be a grand invasion of a new king. Those who were longing for His coming during this time expected He would free them from the cruelty of the Romans.

Instead, the Messiah was born to a young girl who was not married and who gave birth to Him in a place far from her home. Only those who were carefully watching for the signs of His appearance were aware of His entrance into the earth.

His coming in such a way would be our first clue that the Kingdom of God will come to us in unexpected ways, in quiet, unassuming ways. But just because God's reign comes this way does not mean it does not come with power. These two parables indicate that God's Kingdom, once received, will grow, and will bear greater and greater influence over those who have said, "Yes" to its entrance into their lives.

A mustard seed is one of the tiniest seeds, but the mustard tree is large and sturdy, growing to a size of 20 feet, both tall and wide. And for any who are bread bakers, you know that a couple tablespoons of yeast can bake enough bread for your family. The things that start small in God's Kingdom have huge potential. We must not forget that!

I say "potential" because our spiritual growth depends upon our continuing to say "yes" to God. If He asks something of us, do we respond positively? Or do we argue, missing an opportunity to partner with Him by bringing Heaven to earth?

And it is our responsibility and honor to bring God's Kingdom to the earth. We are "brand ambassadors" for God's Kingdom. In what ways may we bring His Kingdom? Do we "demonstrate the products" of the Kingdom so that we have many stories to tell? What might it look like to "demonstrate the products" of God's Kingdom?

When we have faith in God's Words and follow our faith with obedience, we are showing Him to the world. I've heard it said that if Jesus' followers walk around looking like bulldogs baptized in lemon juice, no one would want to imitate our lives! I know that's a funny picture.

I'm not saying we live lives of ease with no trouble. The Bible tells us we will have trouble but that we are to be of good cheer because Jesus has overcome the things in the world. (John 16:33)

So, let's not forget that our small faith will have a great impact. When stretched through our continued obedience, it can grow into a great tree or produce bread that will feed many. As I love to say, "There's adventure ahead!" So grab your backpack, and let's get to trekking!

# Day 100

## Be Strong and Courageous

Deuteronomy 34 – Joshua 2 / Luke 13:22-14:6
Psalm 79 / Proverbs 12:26

Joshua was told three times by God and once by the men of the tribes of Reuben, Gad, and the half-tribe of Manasseh, to be strong and courageous! This was all written within a 10-verse portion in Joshua chapter 1. Why do you suppose God wanted Joshua to hear this message four times? While I can't answer that for sure, let's explore one possibility.

Let's first look at the meaning of the words strong and courageous, then let's look at the meaning of the number four. Then, I want to relay to you a word the Lord spoke to me while I was writing this. And yes, it all ties together!

> The word "strong" is defined as "to tie fast, to bind bonds strongly, to gird." This is not the complete definition; there was much more, but this is the portion of the definition I want to explore.

> The word "courageous" is defined as "to be alert, firm and strong. Also, to be strong in the feet or swift-footed." Again, there is much more to this definition, but this will allow us to explore where the Holy Spirit is leading.

> The number four carries a meaning of "authority, government, rule, dominion, completeness."

I'm sure following in the footsteps of Moses as the leader of Israel was intimidating, to say the least! Moses had seen God face to face. It says in Deuteronomy 34:6, "The LORD buried him (Moses) in a valley near Beth-Peor in Moab, but to this day, no one knows the exact place."

God talked to Moses face to face. God buried Moses. And now Joshua is appointed by God to take over leadership. I'd say Joshua needed these four reminders to be strong and courageous while following in the footsteps of his powerful predecessor. What was being spoken to him as he heard these words?

When I read the definition of the word strong, I thought of a warrior putting on his armor, taking up his shield, and fastening the belt that held his sword. He was preparing for a battle.

When I read the meaning of the word courageous, I thought of a skilled warrior who is unafraid and handles his weapons with great dexterity. Remember, by now, Joshua is about 80 years old! Can you imagine a man of this age leading the warriors of Israel into a physically demanding battle?

Then, we look at the meaning of the number four. God reminds Joshua that He has given him authority; He has appointed Joshua to rule over His people and help them take the land they were promised many years ago.

They were finally walking in the fulfillment of the words spoken all those years ago to Abraham. I'm sure it was surreal for all of them; the words were now reality. The promise was now seen with their own eyes.

During a prayer call I once led in preparation for a class I hosted based on the book *The Best Yes* by Lysa Terkeurst, I received an unexpected blessing! As we took turns praying for one another, a friend said she heard the Lord speak a word for me. That word was "sure-footed."

The definition of the word "sure-footed" is "unlikely to stumble or slip, confident and competent." I was immediately reminded of Caleb, one of my personal heroes.

I'm not as far along in years as Caleb was when he entered the land God promised, but God has continued to lead me into new things, even as I am in the decade of my 60s at this writing. There are times I wonder why I'm beginning these new things later in life, but God keeps assuring me I have many years left to "fight."

So, I, like Caleb, will be strong and courageous. I will be sure-footed and dress myself daily in the armor of God. I will use my authority in the places God has promised to me, and I will remain firm, alert, and strong.

What has God promised you? There is still time to be strong and courageous, and to walk in the places He has for you. I bless you today with the strength and the courage to go where He leads and to make a lasting impact on the world around you!

# Day 101

## *Do You Have God in a Box?*

Joshua 3-4 / Luke 14:7-35 / Psalm 80 / Proverbs 12:27-28

In the book of Joshua, the people of God are preparing to cross the Jordan River and move into position to attack Jericho. The long-awaited day to receive the promise of entering this new land has finally arrived! I know they were excited but probably also apprehensive because of the battles ahead.

But pay attention to whom led the people in crossing the river, the Levitical priests. However, the priests were not "alone"; they were carrying the Ark of the Covenant of the Lord, which housed the presence of God in those days. God was going with them!

I had a couple of interesting thoughts. First, God's people were carrying Him in a box. Since these events occurred pre-cross, God's Spirit could not yet live within His people. Why? Because a holy God will not inhabit, much less come near an imperfect and sin-filled vessel. It is not until we're purified through faith in Jesus Christ that the Holy Spirit comes to live within us.

Until this time, God had been seen as both a cloud by day and a pillar of fire by night. Once the temple was completed, God's presence rested above the mercy seat of the Ark. I don't know why it seemed so odd to me to consider that God had been "placed in a box." I don't believe it's where God preferred to be, but it was necessary because God wanted to be near His people. He wanted to lead them into battle and victory.

That had me wondering. Now that God no longer lives "in a box" but within His people, within His Church, why do we keep

Him in that box? What do I mean by that? I believe we keep Him in a box with our boxed or small thinking.

God is all-powerful and all-knowing. He created all the universe, so what makes us think He can be contained or managed? He cannot. He chose to dwell in the ark, just as He chose to come to earth as a man.

How often do we allow God to choose how He will show up in our lives? Or how often do we allow our expectations to dictate what God can and cannot do? Humans are comfortable with things that are manageable and expected. But our Great and Mighty God is anything but manageable and predictable!

Have you allowed God to do whatever He wants in your life? In a day, a week, a year, a season? In your church gatherings? I must wonder how different these scenarios might look if God had His way. Since He is good, we can be assured that by allowing Him to be "unboxed," we would see and hear things we had not previously seen or heard. He wants to bless us with amazing and good things!

Who's up for that? I am! In our Sunday services, that's exactly what we do. We have a format and an idea of a plan each week, but we leave lots of space for Holy Spirit to do as He pleases. Things don't always turn out the way we expect (honestly, they rarely do!), but the result is much better than we anticipated! I'll take that any day.

Why are we afraid to give God the reigns of our lives and gatherings? What are we fearful He might do? What if we don't end on time? What if the preacher has no time to speak? What if... fill in the blank.

On the other hand, what if God has His way and people are healed? Or salvation comes? Or a new song is written, or a verse is laid on someone's heart to share and it totally changes someone's life? The possibilities are endless when we allow God to have His way. This is how I've always longed to experience church.

We want to say, "Yes, Lord, do whatever you want. We will make room for You. We will submit to You. We will let You be in charge. Where do you want to go?"

I promise, you'll never regret the decision to let God out of that box!

# Day 102

## Our True Identity

Joshua 5:1-7:15 / Luke 15 / Psalm 81 / Proverbs 13:1

As God's people prepared to destroy Jericho, not yet knowing what it would look like to have God fighting for them, God asked something of the men. Jewish custom and covenant stated that the baby boys would be circumcised on the 8th day after their birth as a sign of God's covenant with them, along with their willingness to obey Him and be His people.

Since leaving Egypt, none of the males had followed that covenant, and God asked Joshua to circumcise all the males before they went into battle, thus renewing their willingness to obey Him and be called by His Name.

As I researched, I found an interesting fact I had never considered. Pharaoh's daughter would have known immediately that Moses was an Israelite because he would have been circumcised when she found him. So, she knew from the beginning who he was.

Once the covenant was renewed, God said this to them as quoted in Joshua 5:9 "'Today I have rolled away the shame of your slavery in Egypt.' So that place (where they camped) has been called Gilgal to this day." Gilgal means to "roll away."

Their shame of slavery was removed. This reminds me of what Jesus did through His death on the cross. He wiped away the shame of our slavery to sin. We are no longer sinners, but children of the Most High God. We are no longer part of the kingdom of darkness, but we are the righteousness of God through Jesus Christ.

During one of our house church gatherings, we talked about

the fact that our shame has been removed and that our sins are no longer remembered. Along with that, we talked about how important our words are. We must remember to identify ourselves by the New Covenant and not our old sin nature.

1 John 1:7 TPT "But if we keep living in the pure light that surrounds Him, we share unbroken fellowship with one another, and the blood of Jesus, His Son, continually cleanses us from all sin."

Romans 6:6 TPT "Could it be any clearer that our former identity is now and forever deprived of its power? For we were co-crucified with him to dismantle the stronghold of sin within us, so that we would not continue to live one moment longer submitted to sin's power."

Psalm 103:12-13 TPT "Farther than from a sunrise to a sunset—that's how far you've removed our guilt from us. The same way a loving father feels toward his children—that's but a sample of your tender feelings toward us, your beloved children, who live in awe of you."

Micah 7:19 NASB "He will again take pity on us; He will trample on our wrongdoings. Yes, You will cast all their sins into the depths of the sea."

These verses reveal the truth regarding our sin when we are in Christ. Sin has been removed. We are no longer slaves to sin. God no longer remembers our sin because when the Father looks at us, He sees only His beloved Son. We are made perfect in Christ.

We must now identify ourselves according to what Christ has done and no longer according to our old lives. We are no longer those people ruled by sin. I exhort you today to walk in the new life given to you through Jesus Christ, and no longer see yourself through the eyes of the old life you once had.

2 Corinthians 5:17 TPT says this, and it's profound:

"Now, if anyone is enfolded into Christ, he has become an entirely new person. All that is related to the old order has vanished. Behold, everything is fresh and new."

41

# Day 103

## Do Rascals Win?

Joshua 7:16-9:2 / Luke 16:1-18 / Psalm 82 / Proverbs 13:2-3

"The rich man had to admire the dishonest rascal for being so shrewd. And it is true that the children of this world are more shrewd in dealing with the world around them than are the children of the light. Here's the lesson: Use your worldly resources to benefit others and make friends. Then, when your possessions are gone, they will welcome you to an eternal home." —Luke 16:8-9

Every time I've read this story my sense of right and wrong has been offended! I'm not saying what the "rascal" did was right (read verses 1-7 for the complete story), but he certainly found a way to cover his assets, knowing that his poor management skills were costing him his job.

Reading this account makes me wonder if we children of light could stand to be more shrewd, or if our perspective is simply different from the children of darkness. What does it mean to be shrewd? Shrewd is defined as "prudently or wisely."

We know that Jesus would not condone unethical business practices, so He is not telling us to be poor managers and to cheat our employers. I guess that's kind of Admiral Obvious!

One fact we must remember is that the world has a monetary system and God's Kingdom has a monetary system. The two have little to nothing in common. The world tells us to accumulate wealth in unending measure. The Kingdom says to sell all and give to the poor.

Matthew 6:20 says it best, "Don't store up treasures here on earth, where moths eat them and rust destroys them, and where thieves break in and steal. Store your treasures in Heaven, where moths and rust cannot destroy, and thieves do not break in and steal. Wherever your treasure is, there the desires of your heart will also be."

How do we, as children of light, store up treasures in Heaven? As usual, we'll only touch on a few ways. Let's look at a few scriptures for the answer to this question. Remember as you read these verses that not all treasure is monetary. See if you can identify the types of treasure mentioned.

Ephesians 4:30-32 "And do not bring sorrow to God's Holy Spirit by the way you live. Remember, he has identified you as his own, guaranteeing that you will be saved on the day of redemption. Get rid of all bitterness, rage, anger, harsh words, and slander, as well as all types of evil behavior. Instead, be kind to each other, tenderhearted, forgiving one another, just as God through Christ has forgiven you."

"Give freely and become more wealthy; be stingy and lose everything. The generous will prosper; those who refresh others will themselves be refreshed."
—Proverbs 11:24-25

"Do to others whatever you would like them to do to you. This is the essence of all that is taught in the law and the prophets."
— Matthew 7:12

"Prudently and wisely" for us looks different from "prudently and wisely" for those who live according to the world. They are thinking only of themselves and only for today. We are considering both ourselves and others, and we are aware that our treasure is in Heaven.

Stuff or people? The here and now, or eternity? The earth or Heaven? I believe we must make decisions based on these criteria and any others that would come from a Heavenly worldview. Whatever we think we've lost in the world has been gained for us in Heaven. Lose to gain. Give away to store up. Be last to become first. There it is again! The practices of the Upside-Down Kingdom!

# Day 104

*He Wants to Bless You*

Joshua 9:3-10:43 / Luke 16:19-17:10 / Psalm 83 / Proverbs 13:4

One phrase from Joshua 9:14 grabbed my attention as I read it today (be sure to read all the verses from Joshua today for context.) "So, the Israelites examined their food, but they did not consult the LORD." As a result of not asking the Lord for His wisdom, Joshua and all of Israel were deceived by the people from Gibeon. Once they had given their word and made an oath, even though they were deceived, they were bound to keep their commitment.

The people were angry with their leaders, and the leaders were left trying to clean up a mess. The leaders' solution to try to fix their mistake in being deceived was to make the people of Gibeon their slaves, making them cut wood and carry water. Now they had foreigners living among them who were probably going to influence them in worshiping other gods. What a mess they had created for themselves.

How many times have you barreled ahead in a decision without asking God for wisdom? Probably as many as I have. Too many to count with our fingers and toes. That leaves us with two choices. We can either beat ourselves up over the mistakes of our past, or we can learn from them and remember to ask God for His input going forward.

I'm choosing to learn from my past mistakes and ask God for wisdom going forward! Even the smallest decisions without God's guidance can be disastrous. Many years ago when I was purchasing a used car, I had the choice between two vehicles. One was a prettier color, but I had a sense I should purchase the other one. I went with the pretty color and the engine was blown within a few weeks. It was then I realized I should have listened to that small voice trying to guide me.

What's even more interesting about this story is this was a time in my life when I had walked away from my faith, but God was still speaking to me because He loved me!

Even in the mess Joshua had created by not asking for God's opinion, God still helped them defeat the enemies around them. There were some consequences that came with the deal. They now had to defend the people from Gibeon when five other armies came against them. What was not their problem before had now become their problem.

We are free to make whatever decisions we'd like. And we can make them with or without God's help. But when made without God's help, many times there is sorrow added to our decision.

"It is the blessing of the Lord that makes rich,
and He adds no sorrow to it."
—Proverbs 10:22

God wants to bless us even in our imperfection, and He wants to bring us joy in the blessing. Next time you have a choice or decision to make, ask God for His input. Not only does He have something to say on every topic, but He also loves to hear your voice as you approach Him!

# Day 105

## Words Cannot Describe

Joshua 11-12 / Luke 17:11-37/ Psalm 84 / Proverbs 13:5-6

"With my whole being, body and soul,
I will shout joyfully to the living God."
—Psalm 84:2b

Have you ever done anything "with your whole being"? Or have you ever made this statement? "I love you with all my heart." There have been times in my life when I'm so overwhelmed with emotion that it feels like my whole body is experiencing something! My heart is warm, my skin is excited, I can't stop smiling.

There have been many who have impacted my life in such a huge way that words can't express my joy and gratitude! This has happened to me countless times and I'm usually at a loss for words. At times, I've even said, "I love you more than words!"

"My heart and my flesh cry out for the living God."
— Psalm 84:2b KJV

I've been so overcome with the goodness of God at times that I must jump or shout, or both! It feels like my insides are trying to come out of my skin. It is in those times I'm at a loss for expressing myself to the Lord with words alone.

I was raised in a charismatic church, well, after we moved on from the Methodist Church in about 1967. And I'm not saying anything negative about the Methodist Church! I'm thankful my dad and mom had a foundation there! However, I really enjoy the exuberance I've experienced in the charismatic type churches. Today, they call them inter-denominational or non-denominational, Pentecostal, etc.

Quiet services are hard for me! I'm so used to clapping my hands, raising my hands, jumping up and down, shouting, and saying "amen" that it's hard to be quiet when something amazing is happening in a service.

Then I imagine Heaven. Do you think Heaven will be solemn? I'm sure there will be times when we're so in awe of our Lord and Savior that we're speechless.

But once we see Jesus face-to-face. I can't even imagine the joy, the wonder, and the excitement of finally seeing the One who gave His life so we could be with Him! After that, I imagine Heaven will be one large party 24/7/365 (although there is no time in Heaven.)

I think we'll worship, fall on our faces, dance, shout, smile, run, jump, hug Jesus, hug our family and friends who we've missed so much, then start all over again!

And that part about feeling like we're coming out of our skin? Well, we'll have done that because we'll have a new body! But seriously, we'll have a new body. And all the things we've dreamed about, all the things we've tried to imagine, they will be reality. And it will look nothing like we've imagined because it will be so much better.

Everything I'm describing is what's found when reading this verse from the original Hebrew language, "my heart and my flesh cry out" can be said this way: "the inside of me and the outside of me are joyfully exuberant."

The next time you're experiencing God, and you feel an emotion attempting to escape you, I encourage you to let it out! Some may think you're crazy, but God will be smiling!

# Day 106

## Salom

Joshua 13-14 / Luke 18:1-17/ Psalm 85 / Proverbs 13:7-8

Have you ever said or had someone say to you "Salom"? And have you wondered what it meant? Some think it simply means "peace," but it means so much more. It's a strong and rich word.

> "I listen carefully to what God the LORD is saying,
> for He speaks peace to His faithful people."
> —Psalm 85:8a

Let's explore this word in greater depth because I know it will strengthen you! And it will cause you to want to bless others with Salom.

The word "peace" in Psalm 85 is the word Salom and is pronounced shaw-lome. This word is defined this way: "completeness, soundness, welfare, safety, health, prosperity, quiet, tranquility, contentment, friendship (with humanity and God), and of course, peace."

Let's broaden that definition. The word "health" means "to be whole, entire, healthy, and sound." "Safety" is defined "to be secure, tranquil, those who seek peace, a friend." "Salom" can be used to encourage one who is fearful, and to assure him of peace. It's as if we are telling them, "There is nothing for you to fear, you are in safety."

Do you have a friend who is sick or fearful? Speak Salom over her! Our words are so important. When we speak words, we must make sure we are using words that bring life and courage, along with everything that Salom means.

Salom becomes especially meaningful when spoken in a difficult time. We can always speak "peace" over ourselves and others. In this way, I imagine this word becoming a prayer. Since God understands the full meaning, even beyond what I've written here, by us speaking this one word over our or another's situation, we are giving an incredible gift.

I would imagine faith would be strengthened, fear would be discouraged, hope would return. Maybe the darkness would clear so we could see the beauty of the LORD in a hard place. Even in those hard places, God is there. He is present, giving us all we need. He promises to walk with us in all things.

If you have a friend or family member who is facing a difficult diagnosis, begin to pray Salom over her and her family and trust that God will use His Word to bring everything needed to them. Sometimes we feel powerless to fix or help a situation, but the Lord is never powerless.

I'm reminded of 1 Corinthians 10:13, The Passion Translation reads:

> "We all experience times of testing, which is normal for
> every human being. But God will be faithful to you.
> He will screen and filter the severity, nature, and timing
> of every test or trial you face so that you can bear it.
> And each test is an opportunity to trust him more, for
> along with every trial God has provided for you a way of
> escape that will bring you out of it victoriously."

He will bring us out victoriously! That is a promise, and God never lies. Even when the path or the outcome doesn't look as we expected, we know that He is good and that He wants good things for us.

Can the enemy interfere with God's goodness? Of course, he can. That's why standing in faith and prayer are important. If we're tired or weak and not able to stand firm, that's when the body of Christ steps in to stand with us. We are to bear one another's burdens.

# Day 107

## God Smiles when He Sees Us

Joshua 15 / Luke 18:18-43 / Psalm 86 / Proverbs 13:9-10

There are a few verses in Psalm 86 that give me the sweetest picture of our relationship with God. God is both to be feared, and He is also near and full of mercy. Some friends and I were talking in a Zoom class recently about the fear of the LORD. It can be a tough subject to grasp because we're used to looking at fear from a human perspective.

There is a fear that causes me to be afraid or in terror of something or someone, and there is fear of the LORD, which is reverence and awe. We should not be afraid to approach God; He is always ready to listen to us and answer.

As the Psalmist prayed, he asked for several things, and in the asking, I heard the heart of a child approaching a loving Father.

"Bend down, O LORD.
Hear my prayer.
Answer me – I need Your help.
Protect me.
Save me.
Be merciful to me.
Give me happiness."

All I can think of when I read this is my little grandgirl Heritage coming and asking me for something. When she comes, there is nothing I won't give her, well, unless it would be harmful! My heart melts, a smile comes over my face and I want to wrap her in my arms. Trust me, God is the same way!

His love is perfect. His mercy is unending. He smiles and His heart warms when we approach Him. How do I know? I just do! He's not an angry, mean God waiting to bop us over the head for all our mistakes. We don't bop our children and grandchildren and we are imperfect humans. How much more will God give us His kindness and love?!

If you haven't prayed in a while, Psalm 86:1-7 would be a great place to start. If you're not sure what to say when you pray, praying from the Bible is helpful and powerful. You'll be praying truth along with the perfect prayer because you'll be praying God's own words back to Him.

As you read and pray, please pray to see God as He is, a loving Father, ready to hear every prayer!

# Day 108

## The Sabotage of Love

Joshua 16-18 / Luke 19:1-27 / Psalm 87 / Proverbs 13:11

Ok y'all, it's time to put on my thick southern accent for this post. This post is about hospitality, and you know we southerners have some skills in that department! Food, sweet tea, sittin' on the veranda under a fan on a hot summer day. I can see myself there now!

All that said, how many of you were taught that you don't invite yourself over to someone's house; you wait to be invited. Even if you really want to go, you must be polite and wait for that invitation. Evidently no one told Jesus about this rule, because upon first meeting Zacchaeus, Jesus has already invited Himself over for the day!

This has me wondering if I've missed some sort of boat of opportunity! If Jesus can invite Himself over to other people's houses, why can't I? I think I'm going to try that! Who's first? Seriously, y'all, I'm going to be scoping out a good candidate, preferably someone who I know is a good cook!

Not only did Jesus invite Himself over, He chose the most notorious man in town. He wasn't just a tax collector who was hated by everyone, he was the chief tax collector! And Jesus was going to have supper with him. I know enough about eastern culture to know that once everyone knew Jesus would be there at the house of this very rich man, the guest list likely filled up quickly! It would have been a feast!

The text says the people were displeased because Jesus was going to the house of a sinner. I think they were jealous because they didn't get an invitation! They knew they were missing out on some good food and wine! Okay, maybe that's just my opinion. But I could be partially correct.

These people were all about appearances, and Jesus coming as a righteous man was not supposed to eat with sinners. I guess his daddy should have taught Him better because He did it all the time! As a matter of fact, Jesus was a friend of sinners.

What about you? Would you agree to eat dinner with a known sinner? Would you invite one to your house and share a meal? You know if it worked for Jesus, I'd have to follow the example.

I wish there were more to this story. We do know that whatever happened while Jesus was with Zacchaeus caused Zacchaeus to have a change of heart. He gave half his wealth to the poor and anyone who had been cheated received back four times what was taken. Jesus declared this to be a work of salvation. Beautiful story!

Who knows what God might do through you if you're willing to open your home and your life? Love and truth have a powerful way of sabotaging the hardest of hearts.

# Day 109

## *Look Here, Not There*

Joshua 19-20 / Luke 19:28-48 / Psalm 88 / Proverbs 13:12-14

There is a verse in today's reading that keeps being stated by myself and friends in my Jesus circle, so I want to take a closer look for better understanding. When multiple people are speaking the same thing, it's a good idea to investigate what God is saying.

> "Hope deferred makes the heart sick, but a dream
> fulfilled is a tree of life." —Proverbs 13:12

When we hope for something based on a promise given, that promise doesn't usually come right away. God may tell us something and we think the fulfillment will come tomorrow, but most of the time that is not the case. Promises and dreams can take more time to be fulfilled than we wish.

In the waiting, our hearts may become discouraged. We may become angry, sad, or despondent, sure that the thing we're waiting for is taking too long. If we wait with our eyes on the promise, we may experience great discouragement and might be tempted to give up.

What if we instead kept our eyes on the One Who promised? He is the faithful One and what He said will come to pass in His timing and according to His perspective. We humans are a hurry up kind of race, but God has all the time in the world, uh, I mean the universe. And because we are finite in our understanding, we may think the promise will come a certain way and at a certain time. But God knows the best way and time.

Here's another thought, if the promise is going to come in such a way, and at a time that we don't expect, we may miss its fulfillment if we're hanging all our hope there. But if our eyes are fixed on Jesus, He will be able to remind us about the promises He gave us. He might say, "You know that thing you've been hoping for? There it is! This is how I chose to give you the blessing I promised."

This reminds me of the Jewish people as they waited for the promised Messiah. He didn't come the way they expected. They thought He was coming as a conquering king to free them from Roman rule. So, when He was born with no fanfare, became a carpenter from a small town, and grew up with nothing remarkable happening until He was 30, the religious leaders missed it.

Their eyes were on the method, not on the One Who was coming. I don't want to miss His "arrivals" in my life! I don't want to miss the little fulfillments that will be scattered all throughout my history. That's why I must maintain a relationship and connection with Him. If I'm looking into His eyes, I'll see that glint of joy when He's about to do something good for me!

Let's remember to worship the Creator and not the creation, the One who promised and not the promises. Then we can turn around and thank Him for all He's done!

# Day 110

## Don't Leave Earth

Joshua 21:1-22:20 / Luke 20:1-26
Psalm 89:1-13 / Proverbs 13:15-16

The parable of the evil farmers, or the story of the landowner who left his vineyard in the care of tenants, is interesting. I know the parable is speaking in part of God having entrusted His truths to those on earth, as well as speaking to the religious leaders having rejected Jesus as Messiah. However, I want to speak about stewardship as related to this story.

God has certainly given us truths to live by according to scripture, and this body of truth is infallible. Not everyone believes that for one reason or another, but I hold that the Bible is the Holy Spirit breathed Word of God, and I am working hard to learn what it says and to live by what I've learned.

I'm accountable for God's truth whether I believe it exists or not. And if I believe only a form of that truth because I'm looking from a human perspective, I have created an idol. That's why I'm so intent on asking Holy Spirit to lead me in revealing Jesus.

Here's my question. Am I accountable only for the truth I've received and believed, or am I accountable for all truth, whether I believe it or not? That may sound like a tough question. How can I be accountable for what I dismiss as false? Well, I'm not accountable, unless it's God's truth.

Have you read the verse that says every knee will bow?

"For the scriptures say, 'As surely as I live,' says the LORD,
'every knee will bend to me, and every tongue
will declare allegiance to God."
—Romans 14:11

This means that all men, women and children will bow their knee to God one day, whether they acknowledged in their lifetime that He was the way to reconciliation with the Father or not. We don't have to acknowledge the truth for it to be true. In this way, we are accountable for how we steward what we hear and believe.

In my lifetime, I will be guilty of discounting the truth, I will believe lies, and I will be deceived. No one understands all the truth. But there is one body of truth that matters above all else and that is the truth alluded to in Luke 20. That truth is that Jesus Christ is the Messiah and He was sent to earth by His Father to provide a path for forgiveness and healing for our separation from God.

God is holy. Our sin separates us from Him. These are facts. To be reconciled to God we must accept the teachings of the Bible, especially the ones concerning Who Jesus Christ is and what He came to do.

When we stand before God at the judgment, there will be one main objective. Did we believe in Jesus Christ? Or did we reject His sacrifice? There will be two pairs of "glasses" at the judgment through which we may be seen.

One is the lens of sin and if we're seen in our sin, we will be found guilty. The other is the lens of grace through faith, and if we are in Christ, we will be found innocent. That is scandalous indeed.

We will be declared free based on the work of another. What a great debt we owe Him!

What have you done with the revelation of Jesus Christ as God's Son? Have you received Him? Thrown Him out of your life? Or are you part of the company who killed Him, the religious?

I realize these are deep and profound things to consider, but they are the only truths that matter. I challenge you not to leave earth without having considered them.

# Day 111

## *The Beauty of His Throne*

Joshua 22:21-23:16 / Luke 20:27-47
Psalm 89:14-37 / Proverbs 13:17-19

As a prophetic artist, musician, and writer, my attention is grabbed by descriptive language, causing me to see in my mind the picture the writer is describing. So, I was drawn to a verse in our reading today for its descriptive and visual value.

> "Righteousness and justice are the foundation of your throne.
> Unfailing love and truth walk before you as attendants."
> — Psalm 89:14

The descriptive language in Psalm 89 is a beautiful picture! I'm not sure what the artist in me might render, but there's a sense of grace, beauty, and dignity in the language.

And much like Pilgrim of Pilgrim's Progress may have encountered, I'm imagining what Righteousness, Justice, Unfailing Love and Truth must look like when personified. I bet they are stunning!

Let's look at the definitions of these four descriptive words, so we can begin a character sketch for our four "personalities" in this verse. And yes, they are personalities. I've read and watched The Chronicles of Narnia enough to know these things!

"Righteousness" is "a masculine noun that refers to a Davidic King, or the Messiah."

"Justice" is "a masculine noun that refers to the seat of Judgment."

"Unfailing Love" or mercy is "a masculine noun that refers to goodness, kindness, and faithfulness."

Truth is "a feminine noun, that refers to true doctrine."

All the above words have more than one word to define them, but I chose the words that I felt I could use to best personify the four characters.

Let's imagine God's throne with two masculine figures, one representing the Messiah, which is Jesus, and the other the seat of Judgment, as the foundation upon which God's throne sits. Of course, God is seated on the throne. And as God approaches His throne, He is led there by His mercy (a man that represents kindness) and truth (a woman who represents the Word.)

I'm not amending biblical doctrine; I'm simply attempting to describe what I see as I read.

It was Messiah that brought to us righteousness or right standing with God. It is the Judgment seat of Christ that will bring ultimate justice for the evil things done on earth.

Imagine that Mercy and Truth are walking hand in hand, reminding us of God's perfect character, which is neither male nor female, neither judgment alone nor dismissive of sin. As Mercy and Truth walk hand in hand, they are smiling at what's to come. Do you see it?

If you can visualize this with me, I want to invite you to find your own passage of scripture and imagine what it might look like in your imagination or as a painting or drawing, or even written as lyrics to a song.

Of course, we won't know what any of this looks like until we get there, but for now we can read and use our imagination! And in using our imagination, we will find ourselves longing to be with Him!

# Day 112

## Pass Along what You are Learning

Joshua 24 / Luke 21:1-28 / Psalm 89:38-52 / Proverbs 13:20-23

Legacy – inheritance – believing God's promises – trusting His Word – not backing down – not giving up. It sounds to me like we have a huge responsibility not only to ourselves but to the generations coming after us.

As we read in the book of Joshua, Moses has passed into the spirit realm, and now Joshua has as well. The one who led God's people out of Egypt, and the one who believed God when He saw the Promised Land are gone. Those who saw God deliver them from the Egyptians and be faithful to them in the desert years are passing into eternity. Have they faithfully passed along the stories of God's deliverance? Who will now lead God's people?

It appears that though Moses raised up Joshua to lead after his death, Joshua did not appoint and train one main leader to carry on the role after his death. It appears as if the tribes each have a leader, and the Levites have their towns, but there is no one reminding God's people of His laws and His love.

We know from history that the people of Israel eventually began following the gods of the nations they were supposed to dispossess. And God warned them that if they did not wipe out these people, their false gods would be a snare. As a matter of fact, the practices of these nations still affect us today. Our obedience matters!

And our leadership matters. I am not called simply to lead God's people. I'm called to mentor, equip and activate those around me to accomplish their calling. I'm responsible to look around me, to see who is coming behind me, those who will carry His legacy after I'm gone, and prepare them to continue the message. If we are not doing this, we are doing our family, as well as our fellow brothers and sisters in Christ, a terrible disservice.

Not only am I to be growing in Christ, but I am also to be mentoring others to grow in Christ. Both are important. If I'm growing, but not assisting others in their growth, I'm missing half of my responsibility.

We must all look at life this way! We don't exist only for ourselves. We exist to bring God glory and the best way we do that is by obeying and loving Him and teaching others to do the same.

What do you have to offer? What has God given you? What are you doing with what He has given? I encourage you to find these answers, and if you need help please find a trusted brother or sister in Christ who can walk with you.

# Day 113

## *Why Do We Fear Failure?*

Judges 1:1-2:9 / Luke 21:29-22:13 / Psalm 90-91 / Proverbs 13:24-25

We talked yesterday about the fact that Moses led God's people, then when his time of leading was over, he appointed Joshua in accordance with God's plan. Now it appears as if Joshua has not appointed the next leader. Was this because he failed to prepare? Did he fail to ask God for direction?

I lean toward thinking God would have preferred another leader be put into place because now the people are scattered about and are no longer removing the occupying peoples to take the land God has promised. They appear to have gotten lazy and to have forgotten to seek God's counsel.

Was God testing them to see if they would stay the course He's repeatedly laid before them? It's interesting that in Judges 2:1-3 the angel of the LORD comes to speak to them, reminding them of the covenant they committed to. They have failed to destroy the altars of the heathen gods and the angel wants to know why they have disobeyed.

This reminds me that we must mature in our faith and in our obedience. There will not always be someone there to hold our hand. I believe in the model of teaching where I teach you what you need to learn, modeling it for you. Then I walk with you as you try it out for yourself. And finally, you are free to apply the truth you've learned and stand strong based on your own obedience. If we don't follow this process, we cannot mature.

To disallow this process is to stunt one another's growth. Too often, we see others making mistakes and we think we must step in at every mistake and bring correction or support, but mistakes are great teachers. If someone is humble and open to being taught, they'll ask for help when they feel it's needed.

Is it painful to watch others fail or fall? Yes, of course it is. I found several quotes regarding the value of failing. I want to share just one quote with you. FAIL is our "First Attempt in Learning." Too often we see failing as negative, but it's not, because through failure we build persistence and character.

"Dear brothers and sisters, when troubles of any kind come your way, consider it an opportunity for great joy. For you know that when your faith is tested, your endurance has a chance to grow. So let it grow, for when your endurance is fully developed, you will be perfect and complete, needing nothing." — James 1:2-4

Don't be afraid to fail. As a matter of fact, I love the following question. What would you do if you were not afraid to fail? So, ask yourself that question and go do something scary!

# Day 114

## *It's Time to Grow Up!*

Judges 2:10-3:31 / Luke 22:14-34 / Psalms 92-92 / Proverbs 14:1-2

I want to continue to explore the Old Testament story of God's people because I'm gaining a further understanding of what God is doing. I talked about wondering if God meant for Joshua to appoint a leader after him. I wondered whether Joshua had asked God what to do before he passed from earth.

According to what I'm reading, God is ready to test His people to see if they will keep His commands without one leader over the nation. We're now reading Israel's history in the time of the Judges, but God only appoints a judge when His people pray to Him for deliverance.

They wouldn't need to pray for deliverance if they obeyed and refused to worship false gods. But again, and again, they are drawn into the practices of false worship of the gods of the nations around them.

Judges 2:22 says God stopped driving out the nations from the land to test His people. He did it to see whether they would follow the ways of the LORD as their ancestors did. It also says in verse 23 He did not quickly drive them out or allow Joshua to conquer them all.

This is a test! Unfortunately, God's chosen people are failing miserably. Every time they fail, they pray for help, then God sends a judge and there is peace for many years. The trouble is this pattern continues to repeat itself for many generations.

Was it not enough that their ancestors had to wander the desert for 40 years because they could not obey? It would only have taken them 11 days to make the journey from Egypt to Canaan. The path of obedience would have taken 11 days. The path of disobedience took them 40 years. Lord, help us!

This has me wondering what has my disobedience cost me regarding God's timing and promises. Our lives are a series of saying "yes" and saying "no," both to God and to the temptations around us. I wonder how our journey would change if we could see from God's view?

This is not meant to bring condemnation, only perspective. I love these two verses, and they bring hope when I've made a mess of the previous day (or week, month, or year.)

> "The steadfast love of the Lord never ceases;
> His mercies never come to an end; they are new
> every morning; great is Your faithfulness."
> — Lamentations 3:22-23

So, even if you did blow it today, or one hundred times in a day, God loves to show mercy and restore you! God was showing mercy every time His people prayed and asked for help by sending a judge to deliver them from their enemies. Now we have been delivered from our enemies for all time by the Great Judge.

# Day 115

## Protected from Bullies

Judges 4-5 / Luke 22:35-53 / Psalm 94 / Proverbs 14:3-4

"Who will protect me from the wicked? Who will stand up for me against evildoers? Unless the LORD had helped me, I would soon have settled in the silence of the grave. I cried out, 'I am slipping!' but your unfailing love, O LORD, supported me. When doubts filled my mind, your comfort gave me renewed hope and cheer." —Psalm 94:16-19

Did you have a big brother who could rescue you when a bully threatened you? Or a big, tough dad that everyone was afraid to mess with? I had neither because my brother was younger, and my dad was a soft-hearted guy. Thankfully I only remember one instance where someone wanted to beat me up. "The "someone" was a girl who liked a certain boy who happened to like me. She had decided she was going to fight to get me out of the way. I told her she could have him! I wonder how that worked out for her!

My baby brother was six years younger and would have been no help. And although my daddy was no sissy, he was more a lover than a fighter. I felt I was on my own. But when it comes to the enemy trying to pound on me, I know where to run! And he better watch out because God is a great Defender.

Therefore, I love the Psalms where the writer is asking God to help him. And I love Psalm 94:18 that says God's unfailing love supported the writer. I'm wondering what that support looked like.

The writer said, "I'm slipping," so I imagine a strong arm was reaching out to catch him so he wouldn't fall.

Our "slips" are sometimes physical, but they are more often emotional, mental or spiritual. "When doubts filled my mind, your comfort gave me renewed hope and cheer." Our minds are the biggest field of battle when we are Jesus followers. If the enemy can attack in the hidden place of our minds, where no one can see, he can gain an advantage. We must guard our hearts and minds in Christ Jesus.

Please don't allow yourself to be overwhelmed. Reach out for help. Reach out to God and to people. We were created for community. We all need it. We all should take advantage of the support God has provided.

Be sure you're connected to a Jesus community who can gather around when you need help. I've been the recipient of many blessings through my brothers and sisters in Christ.

# Day 116

## God Does Not Choose the Mighty

Judges 6 / Luke 22:54-23:12 / Psalms 95-96 / Proverbs 14:5-6

Let's go around the mountain one more time. Yet another judge of Israel has passed, and yet again the people are back to worshipping the same false gods of the nations around them. Only this time things are worse because the Midianites are taking everything from God's people. They are taking all their livestock and all their crops and leaving them with absolutely nothing to eat. I wonder if God's people remember the stories of His provision in the desert.

Not everyone enjoys the Old Testament stories, but I'm sure you can tell by now that I do! They are sometimes difficult to read because of the violence and the terrible choices God's people made, but they are also fascinating. We've watched over and over how God's people were unfaithful, causing God's punishment to fall. Then God in His mercy comes to the rescue. God always wants to show kindness and mercy to His people. He loves us in our mess!

In the past God chose leaders who were mighty and unafraid, but in this story, He has chosen a man who lacks confidence. As a matter of fact, Gideon has a habit of hiding, making him seem quite timid. He hides to thresh the wheat in the winepress. He hides under the cover of night when God tells him to tear down the altars to false gods. One must wonder what God can do with this meek man.

As of today's reading, the rest of the story has not been told, even though I've read it and know what happens, but the reader is probably thinking God should have chosen someone else! However, one thing I've learned about God is that He tends to choose those who are not important in their own estimation. I believe He does that so the weak warrior will make sure all the glory goes to God.

"Remember, dear brothers and sisters, that few of you were wise in the world's eyes or powerful or wealthy when God called you. Instead, God chose things the world considers foolish in order to shame those who think they are wise. And he chose things that are powerless to shame those who are powerful. God chose things despised by the world, things counted as nothing at all, and used them to bring to nothing what the world considers important. As a result, no one can ever boast in the presence of God." — 1 Corinthians 1:26-28 NLT

If you feel that you're a weak warrior, you're a prime candidate to be used of God to do mighty miracles! Go ahead and maintain your weakness in the flesh so God can pour out His Spirit on you, using you to do huge things. This guarantees He will get the glory as deserved.

# Day 117

## *The Earth Speaks*

Judges 7:1-8:17 / Luke 23:13-43 / Psalms 97-98 / Proverbs 14:7-8

As I read in Psalms 97 and 98, I was smiling at the personification of the earth as it shouts and celebrates the LORD. Here are a few phrases that I enjoyed.

"The earth sees and trembles. The mountains melt like wax before the LORD. The Heavens proclaim His righteousness. Jerusalem has heard and rejoiced – all the towns of Judah are glad."

"Let the sea and everything in it shout his praise! Let the earth and all living things join in. Let the rivers clap their hands in glee! Let the hills sing out their songs of joy."

Who knew that the earth itself had a response to the Lord? The rivers clap and the hills sing.

Romans 1:20 says this, "For ever since the world was created, people have seen the earth and sky. Through everything God made, they can clearly see his invisible qualities—his eternal power and divine nature. So, they have no excuse for not knowing God."

Some have lamented that not everyone has the opportunity to hear the Good News and receive truth, but God in His justice makes sure every man and woman hears the truth in one way or another. His creation speaks, telling everyone who He is. We had a friend in the past that was baffled, wondering how the most remote of men and women could hear God's truth.

I've heard of people having dreams where Christ is revealed. Missionaries have traveled to other places to preach the Gospel. Our own nation is filled with churches on every corner. Those who have ears to hear have every opportunity to know the truth. Romans 1 says that no one has an excuse. The truth is plain to see.

What about your friends and family who still do not believe? Or those who have rejected the message of grace? While we cannot be guaranteed they will receive the truth, we can certainly continue to pray that their hearts will be open, and that God's message will be heard by them. While they are breathing there is still time.

I remember my mom telling me the story of my Grandpa Ball's passing into eternity. As she continued to tell him that Jesus loved him, knowing his time was short as he fought an aggressive form of cancer, he finally responded in this way. "I hope He does (love me.)" I am firm in my belief that this hope was the open door that ushered my beloved grandpa into the arms of his Father.

In Luke 23 the thief that hung beside Jesus said, "Remember me when you come into your Kingdom." And Jesus replied, "I assure you, today you will be with me in paradise."

Because of this verse and the story my mom told me, I know I'll see my grandpa, Earl Ball, in Heaven when I get there! And we'll play some cards for old times' sake! He always called me a card shark.

Don't overlook even the smallest glimmer of hope when it comes to those you love receiving Jesus Christ. He loves them so much and is not willing that any would leave this earth without knowing Him.

# Day 118

## We Don't Have to Walk Alone

Judges 8:18-9:21 / Luke 23:44-24:12 / Psalm 99 / Proverbs 14:9-10

"Mighty King, lover of justice, you have
established fairness. You have acted with justice
and righteousness throughout Israel."
— Psalm 99:4

Justice, fairness, and righteousness are concepts that are difficult to understand because we tend to view them from a human perspective. Some don't understand why God allows evil to happen, especially to good people. I believe God is as grieved by this as we are, if not more so. There is much to explore as to why the earth is set up to run the way it is.

In Eden there was perfection; then sin came because Adam and Eve had been given a choice. They could choose to remain in perfect fellowship with God, following the commands He had given, or they could choose to ignore what He said. We all know they chose to ignore what God said, eating the fruit from the forbidden tree.

That is the event that forever changed the way we relate to God. A separation happened that day. Adam and Eve previously met with God face to face, walking and talking with Him in the Garden. In a moment, everything changed.

Some argue it was Satan's fault, and I'm not denying the enemy's role in spoiling the perfection that existed in the relationship between God and man. He was jealous. He wanted everything that God had, and it caused him to lose his favored position in front of the throne in Heaven. He sought to have what was not his, equality with God and the worship that belongs to God alone.

Adam and Eve were also tempted by believing they would be equal with God. It was the same lie that caught Lucifer, but of course it was not true. God stands alone in His holiness and perfection. While we may not understand why events in our lives happen as they do, we can be assured that He rules over all things with justice and fairness.

We may not believe that, especially when we are robbed of beautiful things in life. But God is good, even in the bad circumstances. Part of that is our earthly perspective. We see only this side of things, but God sees from Heaven. The thing on earth that appears to be a loss is a huge gain in Heaven. That's why I believe we must look at our circumstances from the perspective of Heaven. But how?

We gain Heaven's perspective when we truly know Him for Who He is and not according to the picture we've created in our minds. God and the things of His Kingdom cannot be understood in our minds. We must learn to perceive these things with Holy Spirit's help.

This type of understanding is an ongoing conversation between us and God, an ever-unfolding revelation as we trust God in all things. Are you facing great joy? God is good. Is your world threatening to crash around you? God is good.

One day, when we leave this earth and enter our eternity, we'll fully understand the things that are only shadows now. All the things that make no sense to us now will become so clear. Our anger and confusion will melt away in the face of the goodness of our loving and perfect Creator.

Why do bad things happen to good people? Bad things happen to all people. However, we may either allow God to walk with us or resist His presence. Either way, we will be walking. It's our choice whether to walk alone or walk with God and people. I would rather not walk alone.

# Day 119

## Jesus Was Full of Surprises

Judges 9:22-10:18 / Luke 24:13-53 / Psalm 100 / Proverbs 14:11-12

The passage in Luke is interesting because Jesus intentionally hid His identity from two of His followers as He walked and talked with them heading to the village of Emmaus. I wonder why He did that. Was it to get an incognito summary of the events without any bias of them knowing Who He was?

Or did Jesus love surprises and "gotchas"? That has me wondering if Jesus and His disciples played the game where you hide and jump out to scare your buddy! I bet they played that and several other fun games.

Later Jesus appeared suddenly in a room where everyone was talking about the two who had walked with Him toward Emmaus. And again, He surprised them! It says the whole group was startled and frightened, thinking they were seeing a ghost! Jesus had to have known they would respond this way.

He was quick to reassure them, so I'm not saying this was a game to Jesus. It is interesting, however, that Jesus told His disciples for three years about the things that were going to happen, but no one understood Him. Or perhaps they had no frame of reference for such things, even though studying the scriptures would have given them all this same information.

How often does Jesus appear in our lives and we are either surprised or we miss His presence because we are not expecting Him? We pray for His help, and we're often surprised when He answers or shows up in some way. Why do we do that? Is it because we don't believe the words we pray?

I think it's more often because Jesus shows up in a way and at a time that we don't expect. We have a certain outcome in mind when we pray. It's best if we pray and present our needs to God, leaving the "how" up to Him. What if we instead prayed, said amen, then began looking for how He might answer, keeping our hearts open to all possibilities?

I've said many times that following Jesus is a mystery and an adventure all tied together. If we would view our relationship as such, we might instead look for clues and signs of His nearness and presence indicating that He is at work. I know this much; He hears us when we pray. And He is excited to begin the answer as soon as He hears!

That leads me to a reminder that after we pray, we should expect His answer. I didn't say we should expect a certain outcome; but we should expect the answer. Who's ready to pray?

# Day 120

## *Remembering Bradley on His Birthday*

Judges 11-12 / John 1:1-28 / Psalm 101 / Proverbs 14:13-14

Once again, the Kear family is remembering someone we love. We are remembering the day our son-in-law Bradley was born, April 30, 1993. Instead of us spending this time together with him celebrating, Bradley is enjoying Heaven. We miss him terribly, but we're thankful his pain has disappeared.

I've talked some about grief, having lost several of the men in my life, my brother, my dad, my brother-in-law and now my son-in-law. I think we grieve well as a family. We're not the type of family that sweeps our grief under the carpet pretending it doesn't exist. I believe we give it the weight and time it deserves.

> "Laughter can conceal a heavy heart,
> but when the laughter ends, the grief remains."
> — Proverbs 14:13

Some people say, "you should be past that by now," or some such unthinking statement like it. No one can tell another person either how long or in what manner they ought to grieve. Yes, at some point, the grief must be set aside, and life must be lived with hope and joy, but who's to say when that time has come. It varies with each situation.

I remember with my dad that after the 4th year of grieving, the Lord told me it was time to put my grief aside. I specifically heard Him say, "It's time to move on." And I knew what He meant! The words of my heavenly Father on that day broke a spirit of grief and depression that had hovered over my life.

I'm not saying I don't miss my dad terribly, but the waves of overwhelming grief have lifted. When God spoke to me that day, He brought a gift of healing. God's voice has a way of causing a shift to happen. I'm thankful to have heard God and to have moved into a different season of missing my dad.

And I know we'll do the same with Bradley. I remember his laugh because it made everyone around laugh with him. His laugh was big and loud, and it still makes me smile thinking about it! Even though he carried great pain, I know he had times of joy. But I wonder if he sometimes concealed his heavy heart with laughter. I have a feeling he did.

I'm thankful God saw his heart and that all the hurt is now healed. I will never understand why Bradley left us, but I'm thankful he's seeing the face of Jesus, who loves him so much. And he's experiencing a reunion with his family who had trusted in Christ. I'm kind of excited to see my loved ones again one day.

So, the next time you're in the presence of someone you love who is experiencing grief, please don't rush them. Please be kind, gentle and understanding. Words can be few. Saying, "I'm sorry" is so comforting. Maybe a hug, a smile, or sharing a memory of their loved one would be helpful. In grief, small gestures mean so much.

# Day 121

## I Am Yours and You Are Mine

Judges 13-14 / John 1:29-51 / Psalm 102 / Proverbs 14:15-16

"Jesus asked him (Nathanael), 'Do you believe this just because I told you I had seen you under the fig tree? You will see greater things than this.' Then he said, 'I tell you the truth, you will all see Heaven open and the angels of God going up and down on the Son of Man, the one who is the stairway between Heaven and earth.'"
—John 1:50-51

"Let this be recorded for future generations, so that a people not yet born will praise the LORD. Tell them the LORD looked down from his Heavenly sanctuary. He looked down to earth from Heaven to hear the groans of the prisoners, to release those condemned to die." —Psalm 102:18-20

The connection between Heaven and earth is fascinating to me. I don't remember reading that Jesus is a stairway between the two, although He most certainly is. There's an old song I haven't sung in years that states, "You came from Heaven to earth to show the way. From the earth to the cross my debt to pay. From the cross to the grave, from the grave to the sky. Lord, I lift Your Name on high."

Jesus in His perfection, His majesty and His glory knew we were here, and He knew we needed a rescue operation. No one could give access to Heaven and the Father except Jesus.

In John 14:6 Jesus said of Himself,

"I am the way and the Truth and the life.
No one comes to the Father except through me."

In this sense Jesus is a door that we must enter through.

Jesus came as a Rescuer because He loves us. He created us in His image, making us His image bearers. And He would not abandon His image bearers because we are part of one another. We came out of Him; we belong to Him. I am His and He is mine. We were once separated by sin, but now He has brought us close through His sacrifice on the cross.

We have several sayings in our community of believers and one of them is, "We don't throw people away!" Conversely, we also say, "We don't own people." Yet if you're part of our community I will regularly tell you that you are mine and I am yours!

We are His, therefore, He was not willing to allow the separation to continue. I know His heart grieved and longed for the ones He loved. So, He devised a plan. A plan that would cost Him everything and us nothing, yet now He asks us to give him our all.

I'm sure your brain hurts by now! The Kingdom of God is not understood with our mind but must be discovered through Holy Spirit in us. I'm forever grateful for my rescue. And because I'm grateful, I will give Him everything. After all, He is mine and I am His. Lord, I lift Your Name on high.

# Day 122

## Filled to Overflowing

Judges 15-16 / John 2 / Psalm 103 / Proverbs 14:17-19

I've read the story of Samson many times, but this time I saw something a little different. I've been aware of Samson's willful heart, doing whatever he wanted to do regardless of his parents' wishes to the contrary. He married a woman they wished he wouldn't. He also appeared to have a temper in the way he retaliated when someone crossed him.

I noticed that he seemed spoiled and self-centered. When he didn't get his way, he overreacted to the situation. No doubt, people betrayed him many times. But he didn't appear to let anything go or to forgive an offense; instead, he got even and in very violent ways!

He lived a life full of what looked to me like stress in relationships. In the end, he prayed to God for one last burst of strength to avenge the wrong of him being captured and having his eyes removed. God granted his request, and his enemies were destroyed.

Other than this final request of God, I saw no evidence in scripture of a man who pursued a relationship with the God who had created and called him. I am keeping in mind that we have just one chapter to tell the story of a man's life from conception to end. So, all the details of Samson's life are unknown.

That has me considering my own life. Am I busy doing things without first being filled with the knowledge and love of God through time spent with Him? Are you? Another concept that I speak of regularly is that of a life marked by living from the overflow of a relationship with Jesus Christ. We cannot give from an empty vessel. We can certainly try, but what a frustrating experience.

Giving from the overflow requires putting first things first which includes God, family, friends, and our work. We must be filled with Jesus so we can spill Jesus onto others. Which leads me to say that whatever we are filled with is the thing we will spill over onto others.

Do you know someone who is often angry? Sad? Joyful? Warm and friendly? You see those things in their lives because that is what is overflowing from their hearts. Whatever is in our hearts comes out in our speech and actions.

There's a song written by Brooke Fraser and Hillsong Worship that is a blessing to me in this season and I want to share part of the lyrics with you.

> "Make me Your vessel. Make me an offering.
> Make me whatever You want me to be.
> I came here with nothing, but all You have given me.
> Jesus, bring new wine out of me."

If we're filled with new wine, we will pour new wine into those around us. What are those around us receiving when they share space with us? It's a great question to ask oneself! May we overflow with Him so that when others encounter us, they encounter Him.

 *Day 123*

## How Can This Be?

Judges 17-18 / John 3:1-21 / Psalm 104:1-23 / Proverbs 14:20-21

"For this is how God loved the world: He gave his one and only Son, so that everyone who believes in him will not perish but have eternal life. God sent his Son into the world not to judge the world, but to save the world through him. There is no judgment against anyone who believes in him. But anyone who does not believe in him has already been judged for not believing in God's one and only Son." —John 3:16-18

These are probably the most well-known verses in the Bible. I want to highlight them, paying special attention to verses 17-18. Let's especially focus on the part that says God did not send His Son into the world to judge the world, but to save it through Him. This is not the time of judgment. That time is yet to come. This is the time of salvation!

Also notice that verse 18 says there is no judgment against anyone who believes in Him. Not only does Jesus Christ forgive our sin, but He also takes away our judgment or punishment. We were alienated from God because of our sin. Not only did Jesus heal our alienation, but He also took away our penalty.

"Christ suffered for our sins once for all time.
He never sinned, but he died for sinners
to bring you safely home to God."
— 1 Peter 3:18a

"For God made Christ, who never sinned,
to be the offering for our sin, so that we
could be made right with God through Christ."
— 2 Corinthians 5:21

The just died for the unjust. The perfect was sacrificed for the imperfect. Are you feeling thankful yet? The punishment I deserve has been taken away by God Himself through His Son Jesus Christ.

It's crazy for anyone to consider taking punishment for someone else's wrongdoing! But remember, there is a massive difference between earthly and Heavenly thinking. Once again, we find ourselves contemplating the Upside-Down Kingdom.

In this Kingdom, those who deserve death are gifted with life. Those who did nothing to deserve the gift are given the greatest gift imaginable. Considering these facts, how could I not give all my resources to serve the One who came to rescue me. I willingly give Him everything. And I pray you will as well.

May your heart be moved. May your life be changed. May you receive this greatest of gifts.

# Day 124

## Lift Others up To Excel

Judges 19-20 / John 3:22-4:3 / Psalm 104:24-35 / Proverbs 14:22-24

I am so blessed by John's attitude when he said of Jesus, "He must become greater and greater, and I must become less and less." (John 3:30) How many of us would say the same of those around us? If you are in ministry as my husband and I are, it should be your greatest joy to see those around you excel far above where you see yourself. Unfortunately, this has not always been my experience.

I remember when my children were small that I was praying for them one day. I pray for them often. As I prayed, I was excited to identify their gifts—gifts that were being passed down from the generations.

One of our generational gifts is that of gathering people for the purpose of identifying and activating their gifts. I prayed that God would bless them in the same measure He had blessed those who had gone before them, including their parents and grandparents.

I clearly heard the Holy Spirit say to me, "No! You pray for an increase of the gifts as the generations go by!" I was immediately struck with the weight of what God's Spirit was sharing with me and I absolutely complied. Now I find myself praying this for all those God brings into our lives. I truly want to see those we are mentoring become everything God has placed within them.

In our house church, we are regularly seeing people activated in their gifts and it blesses me more than anything to see the smiles on their faces as God uses them to be a blessing to the body! My life is so full. I look around me each week, pinching myself and asking,

"Is this really my life?!" I am so blessed to be walking in my calling of equipping God's body.

What about you? Do you enjoy assisting others as they find their gifts and callings? Or are you threatened by their success? We must realize that when each of us is operating as called, God is most glorified. When Jesus is lifted up, those around us will come to know Him.

Isn't that the point of our lives? To encourage those around us and to bring God glory? Love God. Love People. That sums up our hearts at Bethesda Springs House of Mercy and Grace.

Let me encourage you today to lose your inhibitions and your insecurities and ask God to help you rejoice when those around you are excelling! I promise the joy it will bring you is immeasurable!

# Day 125

## Fresh Water to Quench Thirst

Judges 21 – Ruth 1 / John 4:4-42 / Psalm 105:1-15 / Proverbs 14:25

When Jesus talked with the Samaritan woman, he told her about the living water He was giving away. He said the following in reference to the water from the well and compared that to His living water.

> "Anyone who drinks this water will soon become thirsty again. But those who drink the water I give will never be thirsty again. It becomes a fresh, bubbling spring within them, giving them eternal life."
> —John 4:13-14

Jesus is, of course, not speaking of physical water that is consumed. He is speaking of the water of Holy Spirit that refreshes the spirit and soul of a person. You know how I love word imagery, and I especially enjoy the picture being described of the fresh, bubbling spring. There is another portion of scripture that speaks of water coming from within us.

> "On the last day, the climax of the festival, Jesus stood and shouted to the crowds, 'Anyone who is thirsty may come to me! Anyone who believes in me may come and drink!' For the Scriptures declare, 'Rivers of living water will flow from his heart.'"
> —John 7:37-39

When Jesus referred to "living water," he was speaking of the Spirit, who would be given to everyone who chose to believe in him. But the Spirit had not yet been given, because Jesus had not yet returned to His Father in Heaven.

Until this point in history, God's Spirit was able only to rest upon men and women: we were not yet able to contain His Spirit, or be temples to house Him. But a time was coming (and that time includes right now) when God's Spirit would be poured out and would indwell any who asked and believed.

Holy Spirit is God and part of the community which makes up the triune nature of God. He is a living entity Who has many expressions within Christ's body. He is our teacher, comforter, and One who empowers us with boldness, along with many more blessings. Holy Spirit is symbolized by water all throughout scripture. Thus, when we drink from Him, we will no longer be spiritually thirsty.

It is important to be continually filled with Holy Spirit. This should be our daily prayer, "Lord, will you fill me again with Your Holy Spirit?"

# Day 126

## You Were Chosen

Ruth 2-4 / John 4:43-54
Psalm 105:16-36 / Proverbs 14:26-27

The story of Naomi and Ruth is such a beautiful and familiar story. Even though Ruth is not related to Naomi except as a daughter-in-law, they have adopted one another as family and have refused to be parted. In this commitment to remain as family, Ruth receives the blessing of a new husband along with the larger blessing of being in the lineage of King David and Jesus the Christ.

Ruth didn't see the blessings that were ahead; she simply followed her heart and her convictions and that brought the promise of God into her family line. I was so overwhelmed as I read of the kindness shown to her by Boaz and Naomi. The concept of the Kinsman Redeemer is a beautiful picture of Jesus Christ and His determination to make those who were not His into family.

For those of us who are Gentiles, not of Jewish descent, our adoption into the family of God through our Redeemer is an especially beautiful truth. God did not have to make us His, but He chose us. Our adoption into the family of God has given us the same rights as the naturally chosen children through Israel.

Some might make a distinction between their natural born children and those who are adopted, but God has made no distinction. This conversation reminds me of John 15 where Jesus is talking to His disciples about the Vine and the branches. Please read the whole chapter, but here is one verse to get you started.

"You didn't choose me. I chose you. I appointed you
to go and produce lasting fruit, so that the Father will give you
whatever you ask for, using my name."
— John 15:16

"I chose you." God didn't choose us because we were beautiful or smart; He chose us because He created and loves us! All of us are imperfect, but the Creator of the universe, the One Who is perfect, handpicked us to be in relationship with Him through Jesus Christ His Son. I don't know that any of us fully understands the kind of love God has shown.

How many of you have watched the series called "The Chosen" produced by Dallas Jenkins? If you have not watched it, I highly encourage you to download the free app and watch. The episodes are the most well-done series on the life of Christ I've ever watched. You will be forever changed.

In season one, episode one this portion of scripture from Isaiah 43:2-3a NASB is pivotal.

"When you pass through the waters, I will be with you; and through the rivers, they will not overflow you. When you walk through the fire, you will not be scorched, nor will the flame burn you. For I am the Lord your God, the Holy One of Israel, your Savior."

This verse from Isaiah 43:25 NASB also fits well.

"I, I alone, am the one who wipes out your wrongdoings
for My own sake, and I will not remember your sins."

You have been chosen.

# Day 127

## God Wants to Heal You!

1 Samuel 1:1-2:21 / John 5:1-23 / Psalm 105:37-45 / Proverbs 14:28-29

> "He will protect his faithful ones,
> but the wicked will disappear in darkness.
> No one will succeed by strength alone."
> —1 Samuel 2:9

This verse, considered alongside the story of the sick man who laid by the pool at Bethesda for thirty-eight years, reminds me from where our strength and healing comes. When we're sick, we have so many options for healing, options that the people in Jesus' time did not have.

We can go to doctors, use natural remedies, and eat healthier. Yes, there were those who practiced healing arts in Jesus' day, but they were less advanced in the medical profession than what we have available now.

However, we must not rely on these things either alone or as a priority. How many of us pray, asking God for healing before we consider alternatives? I'll admit I don't always remember to pray first. You notice I said, "pray first." That's because there is nothing wrong with seeking help when we're sick. After all, it is God that has given us the knowledge and wisdom we have today to treat illness.

It is important to remember who gave us everything we have and to both ask for His help and thank Him. There have been times He's instructed me to thank Him for something even before I've seen the physical answer to my prayer.

One of those instances happened recently. My daughter Abigail put her house on the market recently, needing to move after Bradley passed away. It took longer than expected for her house to sell so she was free to buy another house. As I prayed for her in January, God told me to thank Him because He was going to take care of her every need.

As of May 14th of that year Abigail closed on both her old and her new home. God answered my prayers just as He said He would! He provided! Keep in mind that He does not always answer in the manner or timing we expect, but He hears our prayers and is at work behind the scenes bringing about what we need. He loves us so much!

I can't imagine waiting thirty-eight years for healing as the man by the pool did. But I can imagine how excited he was to receive healing! I don't know why the healing was delayed, but I'm confident God received the thanks and praise for what was done.

Not only does God want to heal us, but He also wants to hear our thanks and praise. When you receive a gift, don't you say, "Thank you"? Of course, you do! I believe there are times we receive gifts and answers from God that we're unaware of. Maybe it would be a good idea to thank God daily for all He's blessed us with.

I encourage you to thank Him today for all He's done for you and for who He is in your life. Where would we be without Him? I don't even want to imagine the answer to that.

# Day 128

## The Lord Himself Fights for Me

1 Samuel 2:22-4 / John 5:24-47 / Psalm 106:1-12 / Proverbs 14:30-31

As I've read the Old Testament, I've been noticing a name for the Lord that is intriguing me, especially since my current declaration from the Lord is "The Lord Himself fights for me." The name of God I'm referring to is "The Lord of Heaven's Armies" or "Yahweh Sabaoth."

For as long as I can remember I've been a warrior in the Spirit. I've spoken of it several times in my writing and in my life. My daddy was also a warrior. As a matter of fact, when I spoke at his memorial service, I began his eulogy this way:

"At the age of 78, on October 3, 2016, the great warrior returned home. He entered into his rest. His battles have been fought, they have been won, and his reward has begun."

I love movies with the theme of good versus evil, especially when good triumphs, because as followers of Jesus Christ, we already know the end of our story. Jesus spoke of it on the cross when He said, "It is finished." That means we win!

I don't enjoy violence or killing, but I do love a good battle with a shout of victory at the end! I love to imagine myself vanquishing enemies from my life and the lives of those I love. Therefore, when I pray for myself and my family, I love asking God for the angels to be posted at my boundaries to help with the battles at hand.

Speaking of my boundaries, the Lord recently expanded my

vision of what my boundaries include. As I prayed one day, I imagined a line around my property and around the property of my daughters' homes (our son lives here, so he's covered.)

During my prayer time, Holy Spirit instructed me that my boundaries were not linear, but that they also included the air around me to the highest point in the Heavens and the lowest depths of the earth. Talk about expansion of one's boundaries! Right away, I was struck with the revelation that my territory is much larger than I knew!

The concept that has been harder for me to walk in is the one that my declaration is teaching me, and that is that the Lord fights for me.

Scripture tells us to "be still and see the salvation of the Lord" (Exodus 14:13.) It also tells us that He is our strong tower and shield (throughout the book of Psalms.) It tells us that we are hidden under the shadow of His wings (Psalm 17:8.) Yes, we are told to put on our armor (Ephesians 6:10), so I think there are times when we must battle, as well as times when we must rest. The Lord is clearly calling me into a season of resting from battles, allowing Him to do the fighting.

That doesn't mean I won't pray and worship because prayer and worship have been my greatest places of battle and victory. Of course, I will! This is more about a mindset shift for me, and I'm very willing to allow the Lord to teach me to hide in Him.

I think it's going to become more necessary for me to hide in Him in the coming days. I get a sense that a storm is brewing and the best place for a daughter of the King to be in a storm is in the Stronghold.

Will you join me there? I have a feeling we'll be thankful for the friendly faces around us.

# Day 129

## A War of the Gods

1 Samuel 5-7 / John 6:1-21
Psalm 106:13-31 / Proverbs 14:32-33

I've found another passage of scripture that makes me laugh, but it's also bewildering. I'm speaking about the beginning of 1 Samuel 5 and the account of the Philistines having captured and kept the Ark of the LORD. I guess they saw it as nothing more than an ornate artifact, probably worth a lot of money since it was fully covered in gold.

What they may not have been fully aware of was that it housed God's presence between the cherubim. The previous chapters in 1 Samuel told us the Lord of the Armies of Heaven was sitting upon the ark in that place. The Philistines had unwittingly invited a Mighty Warrior and Commander with unlimited power and authority into the place where they lived. Big mistake!

They soon found out that the Ark of the God of Israel was a threat to their lives! But first the funny part. It appears they at least knew the artifact was religious in nature, so they housed it in the temple of their own god Dagon in the city of Ashdod. The next morning is when the funny part begins. Their god – just a statue sitting in their temple – was found face down on the ground in front of the ark.

So, they placed the statue upright again. It's a good indicator that your god has no power if you must pick it up off the ground. I wonder why they didn't think of that! Again, the next morning Dagon is bowing on the ground before the real God, and this time both of his hands and his head are broken off. Hmm, it seems the God of

Israel has defeated the god of the Philistines. I think I would have at least considered switching my allegiance.

Not only did the God of Israel knock over Dagon, but He also brought a disease and rats into the town, showing His power over man and nature. It was at this point the Philistines decided they had better do something and get the ark out of their city. I don't know why they thought it would be any better for the next city to house the Ark. Or perhaps they didn't care, but simply wanted to save themselves.

The Ark finally made its way back to Israel. This account in history had me wondering if anyone who saw what was happening even questioned whether their statue god was really God at all. Were their eyes so blinded by deception that they couldn't see the truth? That's likely what was happening with the heathen nations around Israel.

God had opened the eyes of His people, yet they still set up idols and ignored the One true God. But the eyes and hearts of the heathens could neither understand nor believe in the concept of one God. Perhaps this was God's attempt to show them the truth, but the account doesn't indicate that anyone changed their minds about who they would worship.

Do you wonder why your friends and family don't see the truth? Simply put, their understanding is darkened, and they cannot see. It's not that God doesn't want them to see; He does! But the god of this world, satan, deceives those we love, causing them to worship pieces of wood and stone. It really seems quite absurd to those whose eyes are opened.

For me this causes me to have a heart of thanksgiving that the LORD was able to show me the way to Him through Jesus Christ.

The way to the Father is there for everyone to find, and the name of that Way is Jesus.

Remember He said, "I am the Way, the truth and the life. No man comes to the Father except through Me." —John 14:6

# Day 130

## Our Work for God is Simple

1 Samuel 8-9 / John 6:22-42 / Psalm 106:32-48 / Proverbs 14:34-35

There are two verses I want to tie together for today's devotional. The simplicity of their truth is profound, but not many are able to grasp and walk in what God is saying. The two verses are:

"Jesus told them, 'This is the only work God wants from you:
Believe in the One He has sent.'"
— John 6:29

"Godliness makes a nation great,
but sin is a disgrace to any people."
— Proverbs 14:34

I remember reading the verse in John a few years ago and being struck by how simple God's request was of me. Many in religion believe they must earn their salvation through their good works. That is false. We do not earn what Jesus Christ has provided; it is a gift.

That does not mean we don't enjoy working or putting our hand to a task of some kind. We were created to enjoy working, so it's natural that our thoughts would immediately, upon coming to Christ, look for what our work for God must be. The verse in John tells us that we must believe. Our first and most foundational work is to believe God.

Jesus modeled for us while He was on earth the kind of life we should live, a life of obedience to the Father. In that way, our work would be to ask, listen and obey. Have you ever tried that approach to serving God? I have and it's both freeing and exciting!

What if the body of Christ took this concept of belief to heart? I believe our combined dependence upon God would affect the nations, making them great. If it is godliness that makes a nation great, what exactly is godliness? Let's look it up!

> Godliness is defined as "righteousness in government, in a cause or case, truthfulness, salvation, prosperity of people, righteous acts."

I've been saying lately that if the church had been aware of her voice, power and influence, the world would look very different right now. Instead of corruption and evil all around us, righteousness would flourish. Evil will be present until the New Age of the Kingdom, but we are not meant to allow evil to overflow and rule. We are meant to be the influencers in our culture.

The fact that we've allowed abortion to stand, along with many other issues that are contrary to scripture, ought not be. Maybe we've felt powerless. Maybe we've been asleep. Maybe we've abdicated our responsibility. Whatever the reason, there is still time for us as the church to believe God and rise in the authority He has given us.

And I believe that is happening! I've listened to many who are standing strong in prayer and faith, unwilling to yield to the evil around us. I believe the tide is turning, and I believe the LORD is planning to come with a visitation of His Spirit upon the earth.

I want to be prepared to house Him when He comes. I want to be awake and aware. I want to believe. That is my work. I choose to believe in You, LORD. Will you believe Him with me?

# Day 131

## God Wants to Help You

1 Samuel 10-11 / John 6:43-71 / Psalm 107 / Proverbs 15:1-3

Have you ever felt that everyone was angry with you, or that trouble followed you everywhere you went? When you felt that way, did you wonder what you could do to get away from what was happening? I've felt that way, and I'm the first to admit I would rather run as fast as I can to get away from the craziness!

Psalm 107 speaks about the LORD rescuing His people from their enemies, or when they are in trouble of any kind. I especially love verses 1 and 2 that read,

"Let everyone give all their praise and thanks to the Lord! Here's why—he's better than anyone could ever imagine. Yes, he's always loving and kind, and his faithful love never ends. So, go ahead - let everyone know it! Tell the world how he broke through and delivered you from the power of darkness and has gathered us together from all over the world. He has set us free to be his very own!" (The Passion Translation)

When we're in trouble, He sees it. He knows our pain, and it breaks His heart. He always wants to help us because he can't stand to see us suffer. Many times, He begins to work behind the scenes to bring help, but He also loves it when we talk to Him by praying and telling Him what we need.

"When you pray, there is no need to repeat empty phrases,
praying like [some] do, for they expect God to hear
them because of their many words. There is no need
to imitate them, since your Father already knows
what you need before you ask him."
—Matthew 6:8

See, there's proof that He already knows our needs even before
we pray. Have you ever had God answer a prayer that you didn't have
a chance to pray? Or maybe you just had a thought or a wish in your
heart and the next thing you know, the answer comes! Yep, that was
God! Amazing. He really does love us so much.

So, if you're in trouble, or sad, or angry, or in need, the first
thing to do is pray and ask for God's help. Then wait. He'll answer
one way or another. You could also pray that He doesn't let you miss
the answer, because it will probably come in a way you don't expect.
Who says being a Jesus follower is boring!

# Day 132

## *You Are Never Alone*

1 Samuel 12-13 / John 7:1-30 / Psalm 108 / Proverbs 15:4

All of us feel alone sometimes. I can be in a room full of people and still feel alone, especially if for whatever reason I'm unable to speak about what's on my heart. Sometimes I'm afraid no one will understand. Other times I'm afraid they will think I don't have any faith if I talk about my struggles.

If we're honest, we all feel alone at times. All of us sometimes struggle to have faith, feeling fear and isolation. If we would remember that everyone feels this way at one time or another, we wouldn't be so hard on ourselves. If I'm feeling a certain way, I promise someone else in the room or in my life is feeling the same way and they will understand.

I love the verse in 1 Samuel 12:22 in The Message Bible. It says,

> "God, simply because of who he is, is not going
> to walk off and leave his people. God took delight
> in making you into his very own people."

If God is not going to walk off and leave me, that means I'm never alone. I understand that sometimes we want someone with skin on, which is a cute saying I heard years ago. God understands that too and that is why He has a body or group of believers on the earth. If you're a follower of Jesus, and if you're connected in relationship with others who are also following Him, you'll always have someone to talk to.

Yes, God speaks to us. Some of us hear His voice more clearly than others. But until we're in Heaven, we won't necessarily hear an audible voice of God, though I know some people do!

God knew when He created Adam then Eve that we would long for companionship. His design to fill the earth by us having children is also a component of fulfilling that need for companionship. He knew we would want to look around and see faces like our own. We need people we can talk to, laugh with, and cry with.

God promised He would never leave us. And while it's true that His presence stays with those who are His, let's also remember that part of His presence is found in those around us who love Him. He truly is everywhere.

God meant for you and me to exist in community, for us to have people around who we can call, visit and talk to. One of my favorite sayings is, "Love God; Love people." And that's the proper order for our relationships. Talk to God first (prayer) and talk to people after that (community.)

# Day 133

## Unforgiveness is Like Setting Yourself on Fire

1 Samuel 14 / John 7:31-53 / Psalm 109 / Proverbs 15:5-7

Have you ever had someone speak against you when you had done nothing wrong? How did that make you feel? What did you do about it? We've all had this happen, usually because of a misunderstanding. But when feelings are hurt, and tempers are flaring, what are we to do? The first few verses of Psalm 109 are interesting when considering such a situation.

"God of all my praise, don't stand silently by, aloof to my pain, while the wicked slander me with their lies. Even right in front of my face, they lie through their teeth. I've done nothing to them, but they still surround me with their venomous words of hatred and vitriol. Though I love them, they stand accusing me like Satan for what I've never done. I will pray until I become prayer itself. They continually repay me with evil when I show them good. They give me hatred when I show them love." —Psalm 109:1-5 TPT

That's dramatic, isn't it! But it sounds like something you or I would say when we feel we're being falsely accused, minus a few words like vitriol. Nobody uses that word on an everyday basis! These words in Psalm 109 do, however, describe how we feel when someone is telling lies about us and we genuinely feel we've done nothing wrong.

The end of the Psalm gives us an idea of how we ought to respond. I can tell you that it will do no good to defend yourself, or to engage in an argument. What we can do is pray for the other person, forgiving them for the words they are speaking against us. After that we must trust God to take care of the situation and to be our defender.

In the past few years, we had a large misunderstanding with some friends and as the relationship was disintegrating, the Lord had some clear words. He told us several things. He first told us that He was removing us from the situation for our sakes. He also told us that we were to allow these people to say whatever they liked about us and that we were to remain silent, refusing to defend ourselves. He advised us not to contact anyone close to the situation regarding what was happening. God told us He would be our vindicator. Do you know how hard that was!

We want to defend ourselves. We don't want people to think evil of us, especially if their thoughts are untrue. But it's more important to obey God rather than men. It was more important that we did what God said. Not only did we do that, but we have also continued to forgive and pray for those who have slandered us. Why would we do that? Because even with the misunderstanding, we love them, and we want God's blessing to be upon them.

You may think I'm a little crazy for saying that, but here's a word picture that will help you. A person who holds onto unforgiveness and bitterness is like one who pours gasoline on himself, then lights a match setting himself on fire, all the while hoping the person they will not forgive burns. Who is burning? Who is harmed? It is the one who will not forgive.

Matthew 5:43-45 says, "Your ancestors have also been taught 'Love your neighbors and hate the one who hates you.' However, I say to you, love your enemy, bless the one who curses you, do something wonderful for the one who hates you, and respond to the very ones who persecute you by praying for them. For that will reveal your identity as children of your Heavenly Father.'"

I want to be known as belonging to my Heavenly Father, and I want to walk in forgiveness.

# Day 134

## The Slow Descent into Deception

1 Samuel 15-16 / John 8:1-20 / Psalm 110 / Proverbs 15:8-10

Have you ever found it hard to follow instructions? Whether it was because you disagreed, or you thought you had a better idea, or you simply didn't understand. Have you ever found yourself in trouble because you didn't do as you were told? I realize we would all say, "yes" to this and rightfully so.

Obeying our parents when we are young carries a level of great importance in God's eyes. Obeying leaders around us is another area of submission to authority that God sees as important. Obedience to God is the highest calling toward obedience we have when we belong to Him.

But what happens when we are no longer able to hear and obey God? Is that even possible? I've thought a lot over the years about being deceived and the cost it has upon our lives.

Considering the topic of deception, I want to look at the life of King Saul from the book of 1 Samuel. Saul was anointed and declared king, and God's Spirit was powerfully upon him. Only seven days later he decided to do his own thing by disobeying Samuel's instructions to wait at Gilgal. Samuel was coming to offer sacrifices according to the words of the Lord in 1 Samuel 10:8.

We don't know why God wanted Saul to wait for Samuel to offer the sacrifice. Was it a test? Did God have something further to say? We'll never fully know because Saul decided to take matters into his own hands instead of following the instructions he'd been given. Samuel didn't come within the time he said he would, so Saul offered the sacrifices without him. Things went downhill from there.

After that lapse in judgment, Saul had instance after instance where he chose his own way instead of what God wanted him to do. My personal belief is that with every wrong choice, the deception got deeper in Saul's mind. That seems evident when looking at the argument Samuel and Saul had in 1 Samuel 15.

God told Saul to destroy the Amalekites completely because of the way they had treated God's people after they left Egypt. Saul was to destroy everything. What did he do instead? He kept the king alive, and he kept some of the spoils.

Long story, short; after a back-and-forth argument between Saul and Samuel, Saul finally admitted he had sinned against what God said, but it was too late. This was the end event in a long series of events where Saul did not do what God had asked.

The fact that Saul had no idea he'd done anything wrong tells me that he had set himself up for powerful deception. How did he do that? With his many wrong, selfish choices. Pride had entered his heart, causing him to feel he could do no wrong. He became oblivious to correction, and it eventually cost him the kingship over Israel.

Deception doesn't happen all at once. I believe it's a slow progression of wrong choices, like choosing not to forgive, or holding onto anger. With each selfish choice, I believe we strengthen that deception to the point that we cannot be reached apart from a miracle from God's Spirit.

I never want to be in that place. As a matter of fact, it's one of the things I fear most. I do not want to be so far away from God in my thinking that He can no longer reach me with the truth. I would be heartbroken to have fallen so far from my relationship with Him.

This topic causes me to take a good, hard look at my own heart and to say a heart-felt prayer that God would show me any areas where I'm deceived. We talked yesterday about unforgiveness, and I think unforgiveness alone can cause one to be very deceived. That's why it's so important to forgive the minute you become aware of an offense.

So, do not wait; forgive today. Forgive tomorrow, and the next day and the next. Never stop forgiving.

# Day 135

## Wisdom Built on Reverence for God

1 Samuel 17:1–18:4 / John 8:21-30 / Psalm 111 / Proverbs 15:11

There are times I don't know what to do in a situation. That's when I look for someone to help with advice or wisdom. That someone is usually God first because I realize He knows the best path for everything I face.

> "Fear of the LORD is the
> foundation of true wisdom.
> All who obey his commandments
> will grow in wisdom."
> — Psalm 111:10

The topics of the fear of the LORD and wisdom keep coming up as I read and study, so I'm going to discuss them again here. In the past, I enjoyed leading a class based on "The Best Yes" by Lysa Ter-keurst and we learned that our "Best Yes" begins by understanding the fear of the LORD, along with listening to and applying wisdom.

I also did a whole study on wisdom with a couple of friends and posted our findings as a video on my Still the Mom YouTube channel. Even with all the reading, studying and asking for advice, I have so much to learn.

The topic of wisdom, or knowing how to apply the knowledge you have, has so many facets to it, but I want to keep it simple today so you can use what you learn right away. So, let's do what we usually do and break down that scripture up there!

The word "fear" is defined as "respect, reverence."

The word "foundation" means "the beginning or first of its kind."

"Wisdom" means "skill in war / wisdom in administration / shrewdness / wisdom in religious affairs / wisdom, both ethical and religious."

Let's look again at the first sentence of Psalm 111:10, and state it in even easier to understand language. I will do that using the foundation of the verse, adding in the definitions and putting some of my own wording and understanding in.

> "When I respect and honor God, I'm able to build upon that respect with wisdom. What does wisdom give me? It gives me the ability to know how to handle myself in spiritual war. It teaches me to manage my business affairs. It teaches me to look out for the things God has given me. And finally, wisdom teaches me to live with integrity in my life and my relationships with God, my family and friends."

You may have a different interpretation to help you grasp what the Strong's Concordance had to say about that first sentence. Or you may choose to journal, asking God what He wants to say to you through the verse and definitions.

Let's look again at the second sentence, because I'm curious about the relationship between obedience and growth in wisdom!

The word "obey" means "accomplish, work, act."

"Grow" means "good understanding, insight that is valuable in estimation, prosperity, happiness, bounty."

Once again, let's rewrite that sentence based on what we're learning.

"When I'm willing to follow God's instructions by acting on them, I will increase in my ability to clearly see the situations around me, and I'll be able to respond to them in the best possible way."

I think it would be fun for you to write or journal your own understanding of these two sentences and how you might apply them for yourself. You might even decide to ask Holy Spirit some additional questions to get better understanding.

# Day 136

## Run from the Green-Eyed Monster!

1 Samuel 18:5-19:24 / John 8:31-59 / Psalm 112 / Proverbs 15:12-14

You've probably heard jealousy referred to as the "green-eyed monster." And I bet you've battled that monster; I know I have. There are probably many ways to battle and win against jealousy, but until we do, there will be some terrible consequences of allowing it to rule in our hearts. I want to once again look at the life of Saul as a lesson for us.

Before we discuss Saul, I want to tell you that Jesus dealt with jealousy from the religious leaders in John 8. They were also infected by the "green-eyed monster." Because of that, they argued, were angry, and could not see the truth of who Jesus was. They were unable to comprehend that Jesus was the Son of the living God and the Messiah they had been waiting for.

Saul's jealousy toward David began when the women of Israel sang this song in 1 Samuel 18:7, "Saul has killed his thousands, and David his ten thousands!"

1 Samuel 18:8-10a states, "This made Saul very angry. 'What's this?' he said. 'They credit David with ten thousands and me with only thousands. Next, they'll be making him their king!' So, from that time on Saul kept a jealous eye on David. The very next day a tormenting spirit from God overwhelmed Saul, and he began to rave in his house like a madman.'"

Do you notice the correlation between Saul becoming angry and jealous of David and an evil spirit being sent to torment him? If Saul had immediately repented of his anger and jealousy, God would have forgiven him, and I don't believe that spirit would have hassled him.

What about for you and me? When we notice any of the works of the flesh from Galatians 5:19-21 such as envy, jealousy, anger, etc. we must immediately repent (change our minds) and ask for God's forgiveness. If we do not, we'll end up heading down a deep, dark hole of misery. I've been there. I know what it's like. What about you? Have you been there?

Scripture tells us in 2 Corinthians 10:5b, "we take every thought captive to obey Christ."

May I tell you I believe taking our thoughts captive is a matter of life and death? Spiritually, mentally, emotionally and physically. I say physically because our emotions when not properly processed show up as disease in our bodies.

The religious leaders were so blinded by their jealousy that they missed the joy and beauty of seeing Jesus for who He was. Jealousy will blind us to truth and beauty, robbing us of what God intended for our lives. Don't let that happen!

I want to encourage you strongly today to look at your heart, say a prayer for God to show you if there is anything that doesn't belong, and quickly align yourself again with Heaven. If you do this, times of refreshing will come, and you'll be filled with His Spirit and Joy!

# Day 137

## Just Say "Yes"

1 Samuel 20-21 / John 9 / Psalm 113-114 / Proverbs 15:15-17

When you're reading your Bible, as I assume you do, do you ever read a verse or portion that you don't quite understand? I'll admit that I don't grasp everything I read, and that there's not enough hours in the day to study each thing I'm wanting an answer to. I wish I had more time.

However, I'll often find a few sentences that I can study and find a little more information on. Studying for deeper meaning is not unlike solving a mystery, and I do enjoy a good mystery. Today, as I read all the passages in today's scriptures, I noticed a few verses that I wanted a little more information on, John 9:4-5.

"We must quickly carry out the tasks assigned us by the one who sent us. The night is coming, and then no one can work. But while I am here in the world, I am the light of the world."

This mystery is simple to solve, but profound to consider and I have a feeling you'll feel the weight of your own assignment from the Lord. Let's focus on the phrase "quickly carry out the tasks assigned to us." How many of you did your homework the day it was assigned when you were in school? And how many of you waited until the night before to do the work? Or even the morning it was due?

I'll admit I was more of a get it done ahead of time kind of girl. I don't enjoy the pressure of being behind or late. So, when Jesus is telling us to quickly carry out our tasks, I think we should take that to heart. Granted, if I don't know my tasks, I can't accomplish them. But once they've been revealed, it's better to work daily to obey God than to put off His instructions day after day.

Here's another scenario. Someone asks you to do something, but there is no deadline, so you keep telling yourself, "I'll do that tomorrow." Tomorrow comes and the task is not done. Then the next day and the next, the same thing. Before you know it, many days, weeks, months or years have passed and the thing you were going to do is long forgotten.

But what if tomorrow doesn't come? What if the day you became aware of your task was your last day on earth? If you knew that, you would probably quickly do what had been asked. What if you knew that accomplishing one task would lead to another, then another? Task after task would not be drudgery but would be an adventure where you'd be able to say to God, "What's next?!"

The night in this verse signifies the end of our work. In these instructions, Jesus knew He would be leaving earth soon and that He had a certain number of days to do His Father's will. That's how I want to live my life, with the knowledge that I have a certain number of days to do God's will and to affect the lives of those around me. I want my life to be filled with moments that change both my life and the lives of those I love.

What I'm speaking about is leaving a legacy, and I know you want to leave a lasting impact on those around you as much as I do. Would you join me in changing the world? World change doesn't come in one grand gesture; rather it comes with thousands of small steps and us saying "yes" when God asks.

Lord, I want to say "yes" to You. Will you say "yes" to God with me and join the great adventure? I hope you will!

# Day 138

## Find the Path that Leads to Life

1 Samuel 22-23 / John 10:1-21 / Psalm 115 / Proverbs 15:18-19

The story of Saul has been eye-opening and has also caused me grief. I have been further convicted in the fear of the Lord. In our reading, Saul is paranoid of not only David, but also of the priests who serve God. How far does one have to have fallen to suspect God's humble servants of evil?

Not only did Saul suspect the priests, but he also had them murdered. And not just the priests, but every single one of their family members was murdered, along with all their cattle. I can't even imagine being the person who carried out such an unjust act!

But there are times we do similar things to one another through judgment and unforgiveness. Remember my entry about deception from a few days ago?

Several years ago, I wrote a post on social media discussing what I saw as an auto-immune disease in the body of Christ. If any of you have suffered from autoimmunity as I have, you understand what I'm talking about. For those who don't know, with an auto-immune disease, your body sees healthy cells as foreign invaders and mistakenly attacks and turns on itself. The body attacks the body.

I've seen that happen too many times in the body of Christ and it grieves me to the core! Why would those who are members of the same family, God's family, attack one another? Was it a misunderstanding? Deception? The work of an evil spirit? Unforgiveness? It's likely all of these, but the process of my prayers, as well as reading Saul's life the last several days has been helpful.

I believe God is showing us how one might go from a humble

servant of God to a paranoid murderer. I know that sounds dramatic. The humble person doesn't just wake up one day and decide to murder someone. There is a slow and hidden process that begins deep within the heart, probably without one even noticing. Once that process begins, I believe God attempts to get that one's attention.

It is at this point, the point of God trying to get our attention, that our lives will head down one of two paths. If we recognize God's voice, we can quickly repent and stay on the path that leads to life. If we ignore God in our anger or unforgiveness, we are certain to head down the path that leads to death.

No one would knowingly and willingly choose death over life! That's why this is a huge deception. The enemy is laughing all the way as the unrepentant one slips further away from God's heart. Lord may that never be us!

The minute we notice that something feels off in our hearts, we must get before God and ask Him to show us what is needed. He will faithfully show us so we can align ourselves with His heart again, running back into the safety of His presence and favor.

Friends, repentance is not a scary word. On the contrary, it's a word of safety and necessary course-correction. Please choose the path that leads to repentance! Once again, this is a matter of life and death. I'm not saying one cannot come back from the path that leads to destruction, but how many years might be wasted on that path? Or what if one never repents and all their life is spent apart from God's intent for them?

I don't care who you are, this hurts my heart to the point of tears. I hope and pray that no one stays on this path, even my worst enemy. My prayer is that all eyes would be opened, all hearts would be healed, and all feet would find the path again that leads to life!

# Day 139

## Is This Really My Life?!

1 Samuel 24-25 / John 10:22-42 / Psalm 116 / Proverbs 15:20-21

Have you ever felt unjustly accused? Or even chased down with a false story due to a misunderstanding or even a straight up lie? It's so maddening, isn't it? But what should be your response? Anger? Revenge?

The story of the conflict between Saul and David has progressed to the point that David is having to stay on the run and hide from Saul who is trying to kill him. Remember, David has done nothing wrong that Saul should want to kill him. We've talked about Saul's progression from pride to rebellion to deception and now to attempting to take vengeance for a perceived wrong that is rooted in his jealousy of David, God's chosen king.

David is faced with a choice. He can avenge the wrong and kill Saul, or he can trust God to avenge him. David was tempted to kill Saul, but he realized that harming him in any way would be wrong because although Saul had fallen into deep deception, he was still called by God and anointed as king by Samuel.

Saul is now unable to walk out his calling and come into agreement with his true identity because of the enemy's deception over his life. This makes me wonder if the enemy does the same to us. Does he see our calling and attempt an attack at the root of that call to lead us away from God's plan? I think he does.

I attended a ladies' meeting recently that was so encouraging and affirming of the things the Lord has been telling me. In the past I've talked about how God called me as "Still the Mom." I've shared how my desire to be a mom was attacked, and that I didn't even want children. I've shared about when my oldest was two years old the Lord told us to homeschool, leading me down the path of being the ultimate home school mom.

I've had many prophetic words that affirmed the words "you're a spiritual mom." I even wrote a blog, created and shared on my You-Tube channel, and taught Bible studies. All these things are a direct result of finding my "mom" path and walking out what I know God is telling me.

So, how did the enemy attack this calling? He attacked it with wounding and rejection from my own mom. And this is what our speaker at the ladies' meeting talked about. She shared that the enemy directly attacks us at the root of our calling to try to keep us from our identity and destiny.

The devil cannot stand for me to become all that God intends as The Mom, or Still the Mom. Why? Because not only is my life being healed and changed, but I'm also helping to heal and change the lives of those all around me. I'm seeing direct evidence of my gifting as an equipper and activator as those around me are discovering and walking powerfully in their gifting. And it's the most exciting thing!

For several years, I have operated as an equipper and activator. And I've done so having very little understanding of what that meant. Now, I'm seeing the results of these gifts with my own eyes! Men and women around me are experiencing major light bulb moments, are getting excited about their design and path, and are jumping straight into the deep water with the Lord! And this is bringing me incredible joy!

On more than one occasion lately, either at our Sunday gathering or at the prophetic art classes I teach, I've exclaimed, "Is this really my life?! Do I really get to be this blessed?!" I'm in awe of what God is doing to invade my space and the space of those with whom I share community.

And I have to say it again, "Is this really my life, Lord?!" Thank you. Thank you, Lord, from the bottom of my heart for helping me find my place in the body of Christ. Thank you for leading me to the key that unlocks my destiny. And thank you for allowing me to help others do the same.

# Day 140

## *We Must Hate Sin*

1 Samuel 26-28 / John 11:1-54 / Psalm 117 / Proverbs 15:22-23

Sometimes I wonder if we as the Church, Christ's body, have lost the sting of sin being among us. We can overlook sin, excuse it, ignore it, and sometimes we sadly celebrate it. How are we supposed to respond to sin? We've heard it said we should love the person but hate the sin. I agree with that. But is that response enough? Let's look at a story from John 11 and talk for a minute.

> "When Jesus saw her weeping and saw the other people
> wailing with her, a deep anger welled up within him,
> and he was deeply troubled."
> —John 11:33

Let's first put this verse into context. Jesus's friend Lazarus has died, and Jesus has gone to be with Lazarus's sisters Martha and Mary so they can grieve the loss together. Only Jesus knows this, but He is going to raise Lazarus from the dead. We might expect Jesus's emotions to be sadness that Lazarus has died, and his family is hurting, and that is part of His response. We might also expect Him to be excited, knowing that Lazarus is going to be alive again very soon!

What I did not expect was the response of anger or agitation. So, I did some searching in a few commentaries for a larger perspective on why Jesus was angry as He witnessed his friends grieving.

The commentaries all agreed that Jesus's anger was directed at the unjust consequence of sin, which is death. This goes much deeper than a man having died. Jesus knew He had come to defeat death, hell and the grave.

Jesus said,
  "My purpose is to give them a rich and satisfying life."
                —John 10:10b

Jesus came to make wrongs right again, to bring life where death ruled, to forgive sin, and to restore our relationship with the Father. Jesus was not angry at those who were mourning. He was angry that sin had brought death and destruction into the lives of those He loved.

When God created the Heavens and the earth, they were perfect. When He created man, they had uninterrupted, perfect relationship, walking with each other daily. Then sin came into the world through the satan (the accuser) and all that changed.

Sin destroyed the beauty God had made. Sin destroyed the relationship God had with those He had created in His image, His image bearers. That is why Jesus was angry.

And that is where our anger ought to be directed - at sin, not at people who are trapped by sin. There is hope and freedom available for those who Holy Spirit reveals truth to. Some have hearts ready to receive truth, and some have hearts that are blinded by the devil.

If everyone could see truth, everyone would of course choose truth and relationship with Jesus Christ. So, that must be our prayer. We must pray that those who are blinded by sin will have their eyes and hearts opened by God to receive the gift of salvation He gave through Jesus Christ.

In summation, we must hate sin, and we must love people, even those who appear to be enemies. In that way the statement of hating sin and loving the person aligns with what scripture tells us.

# Day 141

## *You Will Be Free*

1 Samuel 29-31 / John 11:55-12:19 / Psalm 118:1-18 / Proverbs 15:24-26

Have you ever found yourself face to face with an enemy? Or someone who hated you or wanted to hurt you? We've spent the past week or so processing how King Saul repeatedly tried to kill David. And guess what? In our reading, we find out that Saul has been killed on the battlefield. I have some interesting observations on this part of the story, but first I want to put a couple of verses from Psalm 18 here for you to read.

> "My enemies did their best to kill me,
>     but the LORD rescued me.
> The LORD is my strength
>     and my song;
>     he has given me victory."
> — Psalm 18:13-14

In our scriptures today, David has not yet found out that Saul has been killed in battle. I wonder how he will feel and how he will respond when the news reaches him. I'm sure there will be a combination of relief and great sorrow. David no longer must hide or fear for his life. David has been honorable toward King Saul, who God chose to lead Israel.

And now, David will be made king of Israel. The destiny he knew would come has now been placed right before his eyes.

One thing I found very interesting in the story is that I believe the LORD kept David from the battle the day King Saul was killed so that it could never be said David avenged himself. David was nowhere near the battle. It was the Philistines who killed Saul and his sons.

David's honor was allowed to remain intact. If you read the story, you'll notice that David has been living with the Philistines to hide from Saul, but he has also been deceiving them into thinking he was raiding his own people. When it came time for this battle, the men of the Philistine army didn't trust David and he was sent home.

I had never considered what God was keeping David from. All throughout history one king would kill another to take the throne, but God was not going to allow that to be the case here. David's hands were innocent of blood when it came to King Saul.

What about us? When we have someone speaking evil of us or mistreating us, do we wish we could get back at them? Or do we leave that to God? It's hard to stay quiet when lies are being spread, but don't ever forget that God sees and hears every lie, deception and evil action and He will take care of the situation.

He may not take care of things in the way we would wish, or within the timing we would hope for, but He will allow judgment to fall where it should. And it's better that way because in judgment, God shows mercy. When God brings judgment it is always just.

There's an exchange I remember from the 1971 movie *Fiddler on the Roof*. A villager says, "An eye for an eye, and a tooth for a tooth." Tevye answers, "Very good. That way the whole world will be blind and toothless."

Those are powerful words. What if we instead chose, as I've said several times in our devotional the past week, to forgive. Forgive the one who wronged us. Forgive the one who told lies, who slandered or gossiped. Forgive the one who spoke evil of us. Then we will be free.

WE WILL BE FREE

The LORD has given us victory!

# Day 142

## Enter His Gates

2 Samuel 1:1-2:11 / John 12:20-50
Psalm 118:19-29 / Proverbs 15:27-28

Gates are fascinating as there are many different kinds such as garden gates, fence gates, cemetery gates, security gates, folding gates, gates of the mind and many more. Have you ever thought about the fact that there are also gates in Heaven? You've probably heard of the Pearly Gates and St. Peter. Once again, as I read today's scriptures, I formed a picture in my mind of the scene being described.

I'm talking about Psalm 118:19-21 which reads,

> "Open for me the gates where the righteous enter,
> and I will go in and thank the LORD. These gates
> lead to the presence of the LORD, and the godly
> enter there. I thank You for answering my prayer
> and giving me victory!"

Maybe these are the initial gates upon entering Heaven. As a matter of fact, I might believe that to be true based on the clues. These are gates that the righteous enter. That tells me those who are not righteous or not right with God cannot come through these gates. I wonder what these gates look like.

I love that the first thing the Psalmist wants to do upon entering the gates is thank the LORD. Why might one do that? Because without the Lord of Heaven, we would not be allowed entrance. In

John 12:27 Jesus is aware that the time for Him to suffer on the cross is close and He is deeply troubled. He knows what must happen and why, but I know He dreaded the process.

In verse 27 Jesus asks, "Should I pray, 'Father, save me from this hour?' But this is the very reason I came! Father, bring glory to Your name."

Jesus knows that without His death on the cross, followed by His defeat of the devil and His resurrection, we cannot enter those gates that lead to the presence of the LORD. And that is the very place He loves for us to come meet Him!

No, we don't have to wait until we get to Heaven to enter the gates of His presence. There are many verses in the Psalms that talk about entering His gates and that is something we can experience now, while we live on earth.

Now we enter by His Spirit; one day we will enter in our glorified bodies. And once again, I'm wondering what the gates look like. What does the path to His presence look like? And once we get there and we have entered His presence, I'm confident we will be thanking Him. What a beautiful experience that will be!

Are you ready to make that trip through the gates, down the path and into His presence? I am!

# Day 143

*I Love a God Adventure!*

2 Samuel 2:12-3:39 / John 13:1-30 / Psalm 119:1-16 / Proverbs 15:29-30

Have you ever met someone who calls himself a Christian, but seems miserable, sad or angry all the time? I've met some grumpy Christians. I'm not talking about someone who's having a bad day as we all do. I have tons of grace for bad days! I'm talking about the person that you spend time getting to know and they just can't seem to have a good day.

Aren't Christians supposed to be grateful that their sins are forgiven and that they belong to Christ? Yes, they are. None of this negates a bad day or a bad season. We all have seasons that are long and hard, and seasons that are sweet and rewarding. But at the core, I'm joyful, not because my life is perfect, but because I have been made right with God.

That's part of why I enjoyed Psalm 119:1-2 which says,

"Joyful are people of integrity, who follow the instructions
of the LORD. Joyful are those who obey his laws
and search for him with all their hearts."

The word "joyful" also means "happy" and "blessed." People of integrity are those who do what is right, wanting to please God.

Those who don't know God think being in relationship with Him is boring. Can I tell you I've found the opposite to be true? I've had so many adventures since I was born again as a child! For one thing, I'm able to listen to God and He helps me navigate tough decisions and seasons. I don't have to walk alone. Yes, most of the time I have at least one person walking with me, but there are times when the thing I'm dealing with is hard and I feel lonely.

An example of that would be the physical pain I've endured since 1998. There have been people in my life who have been kind, compassionate and supportive, but no one can truly understand the pain or the attached emotions quite like God can. He can read my heart and thoughts, and He has compassion for my pain.

We do our best as humans to support other humans, and I'm extremely thankful for the humans God has in my life! But there is also that aspect of the quiet place in our hearts and minds and being able to totally trust that God sees us for exactly who we are, and He loves us perfectly just as we are. He knows us better than we know ourselves, and He knows what we need to know and learn next to help us grow and mature into our purpose.

We don't always know what we need next! There are times we are at a complete loss as to where to go or what to do. It's in those times we will hear a quiet whisper telling us the answer to our questions. And in that moment of hearing God's voice, we can be confident He's leading us in exactly the right way.

These thoughts remind me of part of the lyrics from the song "Oceans." "Spirit, lead me where my trust is without borders. Let me walk upon the waters, wherever you would call me."

Who says that is boring?
Walking on the water is *not* boring!

# Day 144

## *There is a Shortage of Fathers*

2 Samuel 4-6 / John 13:31-14:14 / Psalm 119:17-32 / Proverbs 15:31-32

Fathers. Father's Day is near this time of year, and just like with Mother's Day it is both a celebration and a hard day for some. Some didn't have a good relationship with their father. Some have lost their father. Those who have a wonderful father who is still with them are blessed!

Jesus said in John 14 that He came to show us the Father, and that if we have seen Him, we have seen the Father. To know Jesus is to know the Father in Heaven. Jesus said of Himself that He is the way to the Father. In other words, if I want a relationship with God as Father, I must go through faith in Jesus Christ and the work He did on the cross.

Jesus said this in John 14:9

"Anyone who has seen me has seen the Father!"

So, if you want to know what God is like as a Father, read about the life of Jesus while He was here on earth. That means reading the stories in the Gospels which were written by Matthew, Mark, Luke and John. Many will tell you to begin with the book of John to get a clear picture of who Jesus is.

God has awakened my heart to several men around me who no longer have a father on earth. There are a lot of "orphans" in my circle. My own husband lost his daddy when he was only 2 years old. His momma remarried two years later. Jeff's stepdad was a wonderful man. But the fact remains, Jeff's daddy was not there to pass along to him the things he would need in life.

Jeff has turned out to be one of the most amazing men I've ever met, despite losing his dad. He is kind, compassionate, hard-working, considerate and caring towards others. He's a leader who loves God and loves people.

Recently as I talked with a friend, I realized that many of the men around me have either lost their dad or had absentee dads. There is a shortage of spiritual fathers in our day, and it's something I have not been fully aware of until recently. Now I find myself thankful that I have a husband who is spending time with these men and pointing them to the Father. I also find myself praying for these men.

A man needs his dad to show him both how to be a man and how to be a father. So, what is one to do when he finds himself without that father figure? God will provide a substitute, an example on earth of what is lacking in our lives. And that substitute must always be faithful to point these men to God as Father.

God is a good Father; He is perfect, loving and kind. He is also One who will teach and train, correct and discipline, leading the men in our lives toward true manhood. And that is encouraging to me, because I've noticed a trend the past several decades to take away the masculinity of our men, to make them weak, even to "feminize" them. This is unacceptable! We need strong, godly men in our world to help lead and be a voice of truth and compassion.

If you know a man who is without a father, pray for him. Whether he is young or old, he is missing that connection and example of a father in his life. Pray that God will send him someone who will be the hands and feet of Jesus on earth, as well as point him to the perfect Father in Heaven.

# Day 145

## *Someone Who Will Run to Your Side*

2 Samuel 7-8 / John 14:15-31 / Psalm 119:33-48 / Proverbs 15:33

Do you have someone you can call when you're in trouble? You know what I'm talking about, a person who will drop everything and run to your side if needed. Someone you could call on day or night and they wouldn't be upset with the interruption. Hopefully we all have someone like that!

In John 14, Jesus is talking to His disciples about the things that will be happening soon. They still don't understand that He will die on a cross, and they don't understand why he would allow such a thing. Tough times are ahead for them, and Jesus knows they will need someone they can call on for help with Him gone.

Jesus has been with them for 3-1/2 years teaching them, being their friend, and in general changing their lives. Now a larger change is coming that has the potential to send all of them into complete confusion. But Jesus has a plan! He is going to send "another comforter" in His place. He's not leaving the disciples without support.

Who is Jesus sending? What is He like and what will He do for those left behind? The Holy Spirit is referred to in the Greek language as Parakletos and the definition of that word is amazing!

This word means "summoned, called to one's side, especially called to one's aid. One who pleads another's cause before a judge, a pleader, counsel for defense, legal assistant, an advocate. A helper. Of the Holy Spirit destined to take the place of Christ with the apostles (after his ascension to the Father), to lead them to a deeper knowledge of the gospel truth and give them divine strength needed to enable them to undergo trials and persecutions on behalf of the divine kingdom."

Wow! Do you have a friend that would do all that? Or could do all that? The Holy Spirit was "with" the disciples before Jesus's death and resurrection, but He would live "in" them after the Day of Pentecost. Can you imagine having a helper with that kind of power and authority living inside of you? Well, if you belong to Jesus Christ, you have the Holy Spirit in this way.

I would imagine you'd need to ask for Holy Spirit's help in times when you sense it's needed. For example, what if you are being falsely accused? Holy Spirit will go before the Judge in Heaven on your behalf; just ask for His help.

Do you need help understanding something in the Bible? Ask Holy Spirit to teach you what is meant by what you're reading. Are you feeling weak through a hard season in your life? Ask Holy Spirit to give you the strength you need to stand strong until the difficult part has passed.

In my other devotional book where I highlight a new word each week, I talk about the word self-reliant and how the Lord is teaching us to be more dependent on Him and on those He has sent into our lives. We are sometimes too independent for our own good! I think this is another instance when we need to be dependent on someone other than ourselves.

We are limited in our understanding and resources, but God is not. God has all the resources and understanding, and He is more than willing to share with us what we need.

I think it's time to get humble and ask God for His help. And yes, that may include asking those around us for help. Don't worry, there will also be a day when those around need your help. That's what living in a community is all about.

# Day 146

*Remain in My Love*

2 Samuel 9-11 / John 15 / Psalm 119:49-64 / Proverbs 16:1-3

Once you read my other devotional book based on a new word each week, you will come to understand that as part of my process in choosing a word, there are times when I'll read a potential word and think of a song. Today I'm thinking of a song after reading about David inviting Jonathan's son Mephibosheth to eat at the king's table for the rest of his life. Mephibosheth has been invited to the table.

Here are some of the lyrics from Leeland's song *Carried to the Table*:

"Summoned by the King into the Master's courts.
Lifted by the Savior and cradled in His arms.
I was carried to the table, seated where I don't belong.
Carried to the table, swept away by His love."

This song is beautiful. It speaks of us receiving a love we didn't earn and don't deserve just like Mephibosheth did not do anything to deserve the invitation to King David's table (other than being the son of his friend Jonathan, who was like a brother.) And now we have been made friends of Jesus, who is also said to be our brother. (See Mark 3:34)

Do you also notice that we are carried to the place we don't belong? We didn't do anything to gain this seat because Jesus paid the full price for our admission, not only to the King's table, but into our inheritance in God's Kingdom. What we have been given is a gift!

So, when I read John 15:10, I understood through Holy Spirit that I do not remain in God's love because I obey His commandments. If I disobey or sin, I'm not suddenly kicked out of the family. No, I'm still His. What I believe verse 10 is saying is if I obey God's commandments, I will love God and others. That's how I remain in His love. Look at verse 17 for proof of this perspective.

"This is my command: Love each other."

This is why it's so important to put scripture into proper context. In this case, if I looked at verses 9 and 10 alone, I would think I had to earn God's love by my obedience. That is false. If I must earn God's love, why do I need the sacrifice of Jesus Christ? I could earn my own salvation. I could make myself right with God. Myth busted.

For us to remain in His love we must choose to love God, others and yes, ourselves. Remain in His love by loving one another. By us doing this, the world will know we are His disciples. (see John 13:35)

# Day 147

## Do You Suffer from "Stuffitis?"

2 Samuel 12 / John 16 / Psalm 119:65-80 / Proverbs 16:4-5

Have you ever suffered from "stuffitis?" I used to have this disease. It was so much fun to go to yard sales, estate sales and sales in general to see if something caught my eye. It seems there was always something that I just couldn't live without! My eyes would light up, I would smile, my heart would race. Then there was the part about bargaining on the price which was so thrilling.

But at some point, I had all I needed. I inherited some of my Grandmomma Wheeler's things, as well as some things from our friend Myra who passed away in 1998. I have useful items, memory items, and artistic items. As of now, I'm "itemed" out. I have all I need.

Now I rarely shop or go to yard or estate sales. When I do, I may see something that catches my eye because of its beauty or historic significance, but I almost always talk myself out of getting anything else.

I'll tell myself, "If you get that, you'll have to get rid of something." And I don't want to do that because the things I have are special to me, or useful for our family. This doesn't mean I don't appreciate beauty; but I am no longer compelled to purchase.

Maybe if David had taken this stance when he saw Bathsheba, he would have averted his eyes and walked away. I mean the Lord had already given him Saul's "house and his wives and the kingdoms of Israel and Judah." (2 Samuel 12:8) In that same verse God told David through Nathan the prophet, "If that had not been enough, I would have given you much, much more."

When I read that, I was thinking to myself how ridiculous it seemed that God would have given David more! He literally had everything he could ever want or need! He had hundreds of wives, lands, the title of king, etc. Why would he want more? But evidently, David was used to getting what he wanted simply by asking.

I believe the problem here was that David asked the wrong person for the wrong thing. I believe what God was saying was, "Why didn't you talk to Me, relate to Me, communicate with Me? I wanted to spend time with you and meet your needs. But instead of you allowing Me to do that, you took matters into your own hands."

Of course, David never would have asked God to give him another man's wife because the answer would have been, "No!" Maybe that's why he didn't ask. He knew what God would say. Maybe that's why he instead tried to hide what he was doing, not remembering God sees everything.

It's interesting how we do the same thing. We think that if we don't communicate with God, He won't notice our sin. He notices. And we think if a consequence is delayed that we've gotten away with something. We have not. Something will come along to bite us in the behind for our actions; it's a law. What law? The law of sowing and reaping.

Scripture tells us this in Galatians 6:8, "The harvest you reap reveals the seed that you planted. If you plant the corrupt seeds of self-life into this natural realm, you can expect a harvest of corruption. If you plant the good seeds of Spirit-life you will reap beautiful fruits that grow from the everlasting life of the Spirit."

David had planted the seeds of deception, murder and adultery and his harvest was death, sorrow and judgment from God. Thankfully David saw his sin and repented, and God blessed him with another son, Solomon (also given the name Jedidiah by God, which means "beloved of the Lord and friend of God".) How gracious of God to bless David again after he turned away from his sin! And what a beautiful stamp of love God placed on Jedidiah!

And God will do the same for us. Whatever it is that attempts to draw our hearts away from God whether it be things, people, or circumstances, etc., let us instead turn away from that and turn to God to have a conversation with Him. He wants to talk with us and bless us. He really does love us so much!

# Day 148

*Jesus Wants You*

2 Samuel 13 / John 17 / Psalm 119:81-96 / Proverbs 16:6-7

Does any of my readers remember the posters of Uncle Sam with the wording "I Want You!"? The picture is a stern looking older man with white hair, a white top hat with a blue band and white stars, a white shirt, blue jacket and red bowtie, all meant to symbolize the United States of America.

I remember this symbolization being popular when I was a child. From the ages of about 6-12 when I lived in Newport News, VA our neighborhood had a 4th of July parade every year. We decorated ourselves and our bicycles in red, white and blue. It was so much fun! We were always excited to celebrate our nation's freedom with fireworks, picnics and parades!

So, when I read part of Jesus's prayer from John 17:24, I was struck by this same message of being wanted, although for very different reasons! Uncle Sam wanted us to serve our country; Jesus wants us because He loves us and wants to spend time with us. Here is the verse:

"Father, I want these whom you have given me
to be with me where I am. Then they can see all the glory you gave
me because you loved me even before the world began!"

Jesus wants us simply so we may be with Him, in relationship with Him, getting to know and love Him as He already knows and loves us. From reading the verse above, it seems that Jesus wants to share with us the experience of His Father's glory. And He appears to be very excited to allow us to see God's glory.

It's a wonderful feeling to be wanted when we're wanted because we're loved and valued and not because someone wants something from us. Jesus wants us to want to be with Him just because of Who He is and not only for the things He does for us. Once again, we're back to the foundational theme of relationships and how important they are.

You're probably asking, "But doesn't Jesus want something from us?" Yes, but not in the way we've been taught by tradition. He doesn't want us to become good little boys and girls (or men and women) so we can look good. He wants a relationship with us above any other thing.

This entry may sound a little bit like a "broken record," but I hope you're getting the point. Our relationship with God is not about our performance; it's about the joy of knowing Him. Yes, that's it. The other things we experience with God are "arms" and "legs" of the relationship. Jesus is the main thing.

When we look for Him first, everything else follows like obedience, forgiveness, etc. We don't have to work at these other things when we're in love, they happen as the overflow of our love for God.

So, let's turn this prayer around and tell God, "I want You to be with me!"

# Day 149

## People are not Throw-Aways!

2 Samuel 14:1-15:22 / John 18:1-24
Psalm 119:97-112 / Proverbs 16:8-9

Have you ever been so hurt or angry with someone that the relationship suffered? Every one of us could answer that question with a "yes." Sometimes the relationship can be salvaged and sometimes it cannot. Reconciliation depends on many factors, and I'll go over some of those in later paragraphs. But first I want to share the verse from today's reading that has me considering this topic.

2 Samuel 14:14 states,
"All of us must die eventually. Our lives are like water spilled out on the ground, which cannot be gathered up again. But God does not just sweep life away; instead, He devises ways to bring us back when we have been separated from Him."

Relationships are one of the most rewarding yet maddening areas of concern in our lives. Since we're created for community, we are innately drawn toward others, including God. We want and crave knowing others, and we also want to be known by others. We want others to see us for who we are and value us for our true selves.

But that is not always possible when speaking of humanity. Certainly, God can know us fully and love every piece of us inside and out. People knowing us, however, is much trickier. We each bring to relationships our strengths and weaknesses, areas we can give and areas where we have needs.

As I wrote the entry for my devotional based on the word of the week, self-reliant, I remembered that some of us are more needy than others. An important truth is that I believe we all need to be taught to depend upon God instead of pouring all our needs on humanity around us. God is infinite and can handle it all; people have limitations.

How does self-reliance and being needy relate to the above verse? I love the phrases where God's heart is not just to sweep life away. But He instead devises ways to bring us back. In other words, God does not treat us as a "throw-away." He sees us as His valuable and loved creation and He will do everything He can to reconcile us to Himself.

God sent His Son Jesus to pay the price for our separation from Him that was caused by our sin. The price paid was His shed blood, and that price was enough. Now we have a choice. We may choose whether we will be in a relationship with God. However, He has already made Himself clear on the subject; He desires reconciliation with us.

And reconciling with God is good, right, and safe because He will not harm us. So, be reconciled to God! Reconciliation with people is more intricate. Not every person is "safe" for our emotional, mental, physical, and spiritual well-being. In relationships with people, we always have choices.

We are permitted to distance ourselves from unsafe relationships. We are encouraged to forgive, but forgiveness does not always equal reconciliation. Forgiveness is for our peace of heart and mind. Distance from a specific person who has harmed us may be for our own good. Sometimes too, if we'll remove ourselves from the situation, God will have an opportunity to speak, and His words will bring life and healing to everyone.

The bottom line is what I've stated above. God does not see us as "throw-aways." He cherishes and values us so much that He gave His Son's life so we could be in a relationship with Him. If that doesn't cause you to feel loved, I don't know what will!

# Day 150

*Cover Me! I'm going in!*

2 Samuel 15:23-16 / John 18:25-19:22
Psalm 119:113-128 / Proverbs 16:10-11

"You are my refuge and my shield; Your word is my source of hope."
— Psalm 119:114

It's time for a good old word study. When I read a verse like the one above, I often wonder what it means for God to be equated with physical or spiritual objects or concepts. For example, God is referred to as Wisdom. In this case we are being told that Wisdom is a person, the person of Jesus Christ.

I wonder if anyone has read through the Bible and made a list of all the words that are used that refer to God, like refuge, shield, and hope. That would be a long project, but I'm sure it would be fascinating. Now, I'm kind of wanting to do that. Maybe as I read through the Bible next year, that could be a goal.

For now, let's look at what it means for God to be my refuge, shield and hope. Of course, you know where we're headed, to the original Hebrew language in the Strong's Concordance.

The word "refuge" is defined as "hiding or secret place, protection, covering."

"Shield" means "protection and defense."

"Hope" means "to wait for, to expect, to trust."

There are some beautiful and powerful promises in these three words! Let's imagine we are feeling unsafe, so we run to the Lord and hide in Him, kind of like finding our own personal foxhole. Once we're hidden in Him, He is protecting and covering us in a secret place where even an enemy cannot find us. But just in case an enemy combatant slips through, He is also our protection, and He is standing ready to defend us.

Let's also imagine that we are under heavy fire from the enemy; he's throwing arrows, stones, and words along with whatever his choice weapon of the day might be. Now we find ourselves waiting for the Lord to come to rescue us. That is our hope, because we know He's coming. How do we know? Because He heard our cry, our prayer, our call for help, and He's on the way.

We may suffer a bit as we wait. We may even incur some battle wounds as we fend off the attack, but we know He's on the way. He wants us to learn warfare, so He waits until just the right time to come to our rescue. Oh, but when He comes the enemy will be so sorry he ever attacked us. He will pay a high price for his arrogance in coming against a son or daughter of the King.

There is also an aspect of our being hidden in Christ that I addressed with a counselor a few years ago, and her response was interesting. We were talking about my gifts and calling, and I told her how I was hesitant to stand up as a prophetic voice because I had been "whack-a-moled" so many times.

She had me stop and consider something. She asked me Who I was hidden in. Then she asked me Who was covering me. The answer to both questions was "Jesus." It was then I realized that if I'm hidden in and covered by Jesus, I am not being "whack-a-moled." He is taking the blows for me.

Any blows I receive have been filtered through Him. That means even though I'm affected, I'm protected. I also realized that someone has a lot of nerve to "whack-a-mole" God. I wouldn't want to be them!!

The next time you're facing a fierce battle, call for help and remember that your "foxhole" and "shield" are on the way!

# Day 151

*The Power of His Word*

2 Samuel 17 / John 19:23-42 / Psalm 119:129-152 / Proverbs 16:12-13

When you're reading your Bible, do you sometimes forget that you are reading an accurate documentation of history? Do you remember that the people spoken of lived on earth in a time several thousand years ago? The stories are real, and the people were real, and they were just like you and me. Sometimes we elevate the people and imagine they were perfect, doing no wrong. That is just not true!

And since you are reading an accurate history, you can trust the words that are written there. Foundational to that, the words were inspired through Holy Spirit. As the men wrote, Holy Spirit was present to bring revelation and to help them remember what they had seen and experienced. That's why a verse like John 19:35 is an important reminder.

> "This report is from an eyewitness giving an accurate account. He speaks the truth so that you also may continue to believe."

The account spoken of is that of Jesus's death on the cross. Specifically, that not one of His bones was broken, as the Old Testament prophecies declared. There is another place in scripture that mentions an accurate account of the things that happened during these times in history. That account is found in Luke 1:1-4.

> "Many people have set out to write accounts about the events that have been fulfilled among us. They used the eyewitness reports circulating among us from the early

disciples. Having carefully investigated everything from the beginning. I also have decided to write an accurate account for you, most honorable Theophilus, so you can be certain of the truth of everything you were taught."

Just as John and Luke have both mentioned, I'm confident every author of every book in scripture determined to write an accurate account with an awareness of the fear of the Lord, knowing that future generations would stake their lives on the truth presented. And that's what we today are doing. We are staking our lives on the truth we find in scripture.

Not only is this truth timeless and accurate, but it also carries the power of God within its words. Here is another scripture to prove that statement. Hebrews 4:12-13 reads,

"For the word of God is alive and powerful. It is sharper than the sharpest two-edged sword, cutting between soul and spirit, between joint and marrow. It exposes our innermost thoughts and desires. Nothing in all creation is hidden from God. Everything is naked and exposed before his eyes, and he is the one to whom we are accountable."

And one more scripture that proves the worth and value of God's Word is 2 Timothy 3:16-17 which reads, "All Scripture is inspired by God and is useful to teach us what is true and to make us realize what is wrong in our lives. It corrects us when we are wrong and teaches us to do what is right. God uses it to prepare and equip his people to do every good work."

When you're reading your Bible, remember that the words contained are both accurate and powerful enough to change your life. Treasure God's Word. Daily meditate on the things spoken and determine to live your life according to what you've read and heard.

# Day 152

## Peace be with You

2 Samuel 18:1-19:10 / John 20 / Psalm 119:153-176 / Proverbs 16:14-15

In John 20:19, 21, 26 Jesus said three times to His disciples, "Peace be with you." Before we dive deeper into the meaning behind what Jesus was speaking over those He loved so much, I want to share with you my thoughts as I read the account in John 20. How many of you have been watching *The Chosen* series?

As a result of watching every episode of *The Chosen,* I'm seeing the Gospels in a whole new way as I read through them. As I read about Mary running to tell Peter and John about the stone being rolled away, I was able to imagine the scene in my mind based on the beauty and strength of the characters portrayed in Dallas Jenkins' series.

I saw Mary's face as Jesus appeared before her. I saw the faces of the disciples as Jesus appeared suddenly in the room with them. I imagined their surprise and joy, and I'm already looking forward to experiencing these scenes when the time comes for them to be brought to life in *The Chosen.*

So, what was Jesus really saying to His disciples as he spoke, "Peace be with you"? Imagine how confused and fearful they must have been since his death. The account in John says the disciples were meeting behind locked doors because they were afraid of the Jewish leaders.

Even though Jesus had told them many times what was coming, they didn't understand what He meant. They thought the Messiah was coming to set up an earthly kingdom, so His death didn't fit their paradigm. I'm sure they were trying to make sense of everything Jesus had told them as well as figure out what they were to do next without His leadership.

> In Greek, the words "peace be with you" are Eirene (i-ray-nay) Hymin (hoo-min) which means, especially when spoken by The Messiah, "the way that leads to peace (salvation.)"

> There is much more meant here, such as "rest, safety, the tranquil state of a soul assured of its salvation so fearing nothing from God."

As I prayed over this, and although much more is meant by Jesus's words, I believe He was telling His disciples something like this:

> "Do you remember me saying I came to show you the Father? Do you remember me saying I was bringing Salvation? That's been done. When I died, I went into hell and took away the devil's power and authority over you. Now I'm giving you the Salvation that my sacrifice paid for."

I believe this was the first instance of Salvation in scripture! Jesus spoke these words of peace three times in a span of eight days. In other words, He was saying to those He loved, "I came to bring Salvation. Now receive My Salvation!"

During Jesus's first appearance with His disciples, He also breathed on them and said, "Receive the Holy Spirit," then He spoke to them about forgiveness of sin. I'm now imagining the disciples understanding the fullness of Jesus's mission for having come to earth. I have a feeling their eyes were opened, along with their hearts, as they received the Spirit of God into themselves.

Prior to this moment, Holy Spirit had only rested upon men and women. Now, for the first time ever, Holy Spirit was living on the inside! And since it's Holy Spirit's job to show Jesus and bring understanding, I bet they finally had the answers to so many questions.

Will you receive Him too?

# Day 153

## The Impulsive Jesus Lover

2 Samuel 19:11-20:13 / John 21 / Psalm 120 / Proverbs 16:16-17

I've often spoken of different personality types and the things I admire about each one. I love the quiet observer who will suddenly speak and the whole room is quiet because of the profound wisdom being offered. I also appreciate the extroverted lovers of crowds of people who flit around the room making everyone feel special. There is one personality type, however, that not everyone appreciates and that is the bold, clear-spoken one.

My daughter Katherine has this personality, and she is confident, bold, and feels free to share her convictions. And let me tell you, when she was little, she gave her daddy and me a run for our money! She was always getting into something, either climbing a tree or tearing a beetle apart with her fingers to see what was inside.

Now, when I see a parent with a child like this, I encourage them to discover what an amazing human they are and will be. I know, because Katherine has matured into an amazing woman of God!

And in many ways Katherine reminds me of Simon Peter as described in the Gospels. As I read John 21, I could once again see the scene in my head. There is Peter out in the boat fishing with all his might, oblivious to the fact that Jesus has arrived on shore. But once he's made aware that Jesus is present, he puts on his tunic and impulsively jumps into the water to swim to shore.

He didn't worry about getting his clothes wet or worry that he might get tired swimming that far. I think he was simply so excited to get to Jesus that without another thought, he jumped right in! And I just love those who are fearless and confident of what they want.

Simon knew Jesus would receive Him, even though they had not yet had the conversation of Simon's three-time denial. Simon was confident in who he had learned Jesus to be and knew He was loved and welcomed. And Jesus didn't let the opportunity hang unresolved. Jesus addressed the triple denial by asking Simon the same question three times.

"Simon son of John, do you love me more than these?"
"Simon son of John, do you love me?" And finally,
"Simon son of John, do you love me?"
(taken from John 21:15-17)

I don't know at what point Simon realized what Jesus was doing, because the questions hurt him as they were asked repeatedly. However, Simon affirmed his love for Jesus by saying, "Lord, you know everything. You know that I love You." John 21:17b

We have the blessing of also saying to Jesus,

"Lord, you know everything, and You know I love You."

I tend to also be a passionate, outspoken, but extremely loving person. I will love the warts off you if you'll let me! I think I'm this way because I realize life is short and we're put here to make a difference, both in our family and in the lives of those around us. Maybe I'll live to that 120 years I've often asked God for, the same 120 years my daddy wanted.

No matter how many years I have left (and one does begin to think about these things at some point), I want every second of my life to matter for God's Kingdom. I want to soak in Jesus and pour Him out on others. I can think of no better way to spend my life.

# Day 154

## The What If Game

2 Samuel 20:14-21:22 / Acts 1 / Psalm 121 / Proverbs 16:18

When I read these scriptures, Jeff and I were at youth camp with our daughter Katherine, her hubby Joshua and our first two grandbabies, Heritage and Oliver, and of course about 50 awesome teens! It was cooler than we expected, and raining, a perfect day to take a break and write!

There are times I feel alone and afraid. As a matter of fact, I don't like being in the house alone, especially at night. We've never had anyone try to break in, although we did have our cars ransacked a few years ago, and Jeff's truck was stolen. I've often wondered why I am afraid. What am I afraid of?

Most of the time I'm fearful of the unknown, or of what could or might happen. The Bible calls that "borrowing trouble." (Matthew 6:34) Jeff sometimes plays what I like to call *The What If Game*, and it drives me crazy! He'll think of the worst possible scenario and talk about it until he's all upset. 99% of the time, this scenario will never come to pass, so he's created a myth of fear by talking about the "what if's."

I always ask him to stop. I figure I have enough fears in my brain without creating and meditating on scary things that might happen!

I wonder why our first thoughts are fearful instead of faith-filled? I have a feeling it's a direct result of what we meditate on. Who wants to make a pact with me? That we choose to meditate upon and dream about good things happening. What if we choose to believe these verses and turn that "what if" game on its head?! We'll call our new game *What If Faith*!

Let's begin our *What if Faith* game with Psalm 121, and I encourage you to speak this to the Lord as a prayer. God's Word is full of truth, no "what ifs" included!!

Psalm 121 The Passion Translation reads,

"I look up to the mountains and hills, longing for God's help. But then I realize that our true help and protection is only from the Lord, our Creator who made the Heavens and the earth. He will guard and guide me, never letting me stumble or fall. God is my keeper; he will never forget nor ignore me. He will never slumber nor sleep; he is the Guardian-God for his people, Israel. Yahweh himself will watch over you; he's always at your side to shelter you safely in his presence. He's protecting you from all danger both day and night. He will keep you from every form of evil or calamity as he continuously watches over you. You will be guarded by God himself. You will be safe when you leave your home, and safely you will return. He will protect you now, and he'll protect you forevermore!"

*What if I need help?*
He will not forget or ignore me.

*What if I'm in danger?*
He will be awake, watching over me and right by my side.

*What if I'm afraid to leave my home?*
He will go with me to guard me and to make sure I safely return.

Now, isn't that form of the *What If* game much better!

# Day 155

## He Enables Me to Stand

2 Samuel 22:1-23:23 / Acts 2 / Psalm 122 / Proverbs 16:19-20

Maybe it's just me but there are days, weeks, months and sometimes years where I feel like I'm not making much progress in my spiritual life, much less affecting the lives of others. Then again, maybe I'm too hard on myself. When we're focused on the surroundings of our own fishbowl, it's difficult to see how far we've come. That's why Christian community is so vital.

Some of our greatest growth happens when we're in close relationship with others. We don't grow well alone because there is no one to challenge our views that might be off base according to scripture. I mentioned recently that someone in my community noticed my life and heard a word to describe me, which blessed me so much!

She heard the word "surefooted" and as I was reading the scriptures for today, I came across a verse I believe God is using as a model for my life in this season.

There is so much richness in today's readings that it's difficult to choose just this one verse. Honestly, I feel I could spend a year just in 2 Samuel, which is a requote of portions of the book of Psalms. After reading 2 Samuel, plus Acts 2 where the young church explodes after receiving the gift of Holy Spirit, I was fired up!

But there is just one verse I want to talk about, and I want to dive as deep into this verse as I'm able using the Strong's Concordance and my own experience and thoughts. The verse I want to talk about is 2 Samuel 22:34.

"He makes me as surefooted as a deer,
enabling me to stand on mountain heights."

Before I dive into the meaning, I want to tell you about a vision I had. In my vision I saw the face of a white deer, then I saw a crown on my own head, but not your typical crown. This crown was woven horns like a deer would have, only they went up and back about three feet above my head instead of out to the sides like usual.

I hope that picture is clear. While I don't have a full meaning of this vision from the Lord, I am sure the above verse is part of what He's telling me about who I am. If He makes me as surefooted as a deer, enabling me to stand on mountain heights, I want to know more about what that means.

"He makes me as 'surefooted' as a deer."

The word "surefooted" is defined as "He levels and equalizes my feet. He counterbalances me and causes me to become like (the deer.) He levels, smooths, and sets my feet. He enables me to endure."

If you've studied the history of the deer or hind, you know they are adept at climbing among rocky mountain ranges without losing their footing. Contrary to our wishes, life is not a smooth, level road. Life has a way of throwing us curves and leading us through rocky places. But if we are like the deer, God allows us to remain surefooted in the hard places.

"Enabling me to stand on mountain heights"
(the New American Standard Bible says, He "sets me
on my high places.")

The word "stand" is defined as "He causes me to stand, to take my stand, to be in a standing attitude, to stand still and stop moving, endure, persist, be steadfast, to hold my ground. Where? On the high places, mountains or battlefields."

If you've read much of scripture, you know that the "high places" in the Old Testament were the places where pagan altars were set up. This is where false gods were worshiped. The men of God, the kings and leaders in the community, were told throughout Israel's history to tear down the high places where idol worship took place. So, using this comparison, it's interesting to me that God enables us to stand in enemy territory as we battle with His help!

When we're on a high place, we're preparing to survey the land, find where our enemies are hidden, and plan and execute a strategy for battle. The enemy is always at war with us, trying to kill and steal from us. So, of course, God strengthens us to stand strong, see what our enemy is doing, and fight in battle against him.

If we do not fight, the devil takes away the place we stand, our ability to believe God, and any other thing he can rob from us. We must always be prepared to fight against his plans. And it's exciting and comforting that God is aware of this battle and prepares us to be strong. The good news is that when we're in Christ, we never fight alone.

This verse is telling us we are going to have battles, but God enables us to stand strong. So, don't allow yourself to get tired. Rest a bit then get right back up and stand firmly in the place God has called you to. Endure the hardship and you will come out on the other side in victory!

185

# Day 156

## A Servant of Jesus Christ

2 Samuel 23:24-24:25 / Acts 3 / Psalm 123 / Proverbs 16:21-23

We're all trying to "get ahead" in this "dog eat dog" world. We're taught to "look out for number one." We're taught that everyone else can take care of themselves. The problem with thinking this way is it causes us to fight against one another, or even to push one another down so we can be lifted.

None of this is living the way Jesus taught us. However, even before we consider the "one-anothering" verses we find in scripture, we must be fixed in our dependence on God.

Psalm 123:2 in The Passion Translation says this,

"The way I love you is like the way a servant wants to please his master, the way a maid waits for the orders of her mistress. We look to you, our god, with passionate longing to please you and discover more of your mercy and grace."

We must ask ourselves this question, do we look to God? Or do we look to people, trying to please them and gain favor from them? If we looked to God for mercy or favor, we wouldn't need to look to people at all except to discover how we may serve them. And if we went about life this way, no one would have any needs!

The description in Charles Spurgeon's Treasury of David, a full commentary of the book of Psalms, is beautifully descriptive of the process described in verse 2.

186

"In times past, servants were often employed by masters of houses to help with everyday tasks. Often these servants were trained to respond not just to spoken words, but to hand gestures. They were required to keep their eyes trained every moment upon those directing them. They would have been scolded if they had missed a cue."

While God doesn't scold us for missing a cue from Him, whether heard or seen in the things around us, we will most certainly miss opportunities for God to pour his favor on us if we're not carefully aware.

Once you are born from above and your entire heart and soul belong to God, you want nothing more than to please Him, to make Him smile. And this is not about serving some hard person; this is about a loving relationship. We want to please Him because we love Him. And we love Him because He loved us first.

So, never think about serving God as a drudgery. The rewards of relationship with Him are far too great for that! Serving Him is an honor and will fill our lives with such a rich sweetness that we'll become almost addicted to the beauty of what He brings to us.

I've been in love with Jesus since He filled me with Himself in 1967. My love for Him grows stronger, not weaker. For all I know of Him, I have so much more yet to learn. I wake up every morning excited to read His Word and discover something new about His beautiful nature and character.

If you don't yet love Him this way, there is still time to join me on this amazing adventure. I promise your life will never be the same! Serving Jesus is exciting! It's been one new discovery after another, and I'm sure there are many more treasures I have yet to unearth.

Today, I'm going to watch for Him to see what beauty and favor He might want to share with me. He loves us more than words could ever describe!

# Day 157

## *What a Difference Holy Spirit Makes!*

1 Kings 1 / Acts 4 / Psalm 124 / Proverbs 16:24

I'm fascinated by everyone's before and after stories. I love the stories of redemption, overcoming, and of good winning over evil. I am inspired by reading about someone's life before and after a loss, before and after overcoming an addiction or having been abused, before and after accepting Christ, and the list could go on and on.

The human spirit as created by God is powerful and strong, able to hope against all odds and move past some terrible things. Which brings me to the point of today's entry. As I read about Peter in Acts 4, I remembered back a few chapters ago in John when he denied Jesus, then Jesus restored him again to relationship by asking if Peter loved Him.

Peter was cowardly, hiding in fear and stating he didn't know the man he had walked in close relationship with for three and a half years. And then Jesus sent His Holy Spirit, giving the disciples boldness to be witnesses for the Good News Jesus came to reveal. Peter was a totally different man after receiving Holy Spirit baptism. He was bold and all those around noticed the difference.

Acts 4 :13 states,

"The members of the council were amazed when they saw the boldness of Peter and John, for they could see that they were ordinary men with no special training in the Scriptures. They also recognized them as men who had been with Jesus."

Even the well-educated religious leaders noticed something different about Peter. The leaders realized Peter had not been educated as they had been, but they recognized that he and the others spoke with authority. Even if they did not understand or receive the message, they noticed the way it was delivered.

As we keep reading, we'll see that the apostles and other disciples continued to be bold and grow stronger each day. They became the witnesses Jesus promised they would become. I would love to have been around to see the excitement during this time in history.

Another proof of this new boldness is that after going before the council, many men and women would have hidden and refused to speak again, fearing arrest, beating or death. Not these men and women! Their first response is to hold another prayer meeting and to receive another filling with Holy Spirit.

And guess what? They went out again to boldly preach even though the religious leaders tried to get them to stop speaking in the name of Jesus. That's some serious boldness! And I believe the Church today needs this type of boldness to stand for truth. So, when we find ourselves shrinking back in fear, maybe it's time we pray to receive another infilling of God's Spirit so we can continue along as God has called us to do!

# Day 158

## The LORD Surrounds His People

1 Kings 2:1-3:2 / Acts 5 / Psalm 125 / Proverbs 16:25

Feeling safe is one of the most basic human needs. If we don't feel safe, we will not walk through life with confidence and we will not fulfill the calling God has for us. However, our confidence cannot be in people or things; our confidence must be in the Lord. People will disappoint us, but God will not.

> "Just as the mountains surround Jerusalem,
> so the LORD surrounds His people,
> both now and forever."
> —Psalm 125:2

Here in East Tennessee, we are in a valley surrounded by mountains on one side and a plateau on the other. There have been many instances over the many years I've lived here (since October 1975) when a storm system was coming from the west, and once that storm came across the plateau, it would dissipate before affecting those in the valley. The mountains and the plateau have been a protection for those of us living in the valley.

I imagine it is the same for the mountains that surround Jerusalem; I'm sure they have been a source of protection for the city these many years. The mountains likely protect from storms, wild animals, etc. The mountains would also give a vantage point to see invaders attempting to affect Jerusalem.

The meaning of the name "Jerusalem" is "pointing the way to completeness." I believe this protected city allows those who live in her both to feel safe and to fulfill God's call because of that safety.

Just as Jerusalem has mountains that surround her, you and I have the LORD surrounding us for protection and safety. He can guard us from all enemies and negative influences. That does not mean we are not affected by things, however, everything that comes our way must first pass through the LORD. In that way, He is like a filter for everything that comes to us.

We must not forget that difficulty and trials shape and mature us into the image of Christ. Therefore, we cannot and must not be shielded from everything that attempts to affect us. Otherwise, our growth would be stifled, and we would never be changed into looking like Jesus. God forbid that should happen!

Today, as you're facing whatever may come your way, remember that you are surrounded. Not by evil and chaos, but by the LORD and His Shalom! He is speaking peace (safety and strength) over you every single minute of every single day. You can overcome whatever happens!

# Day 159

## The Gift of Wisdom

1 Kings 3:3-4:34 / Acts 6 / Psalm 126 / Proverbs 16:26-27

Have you ever tried to give someone something then realized you couldn't find that thing? Or that you were out of whatever item you wanted to give? Just as we cannot give what we do not physically possess, we cannot give what we do not spiritually possess. The example I'm considering today is wisdom. How can I give someone wisdom when I don't have wisdom? Well, I can't!

I have been blessed to hear God speaking to me since I was born again as a little girl. I easily hear from God's Spirit and He has shared many things with me. I've heard encouraging words for myself and for others, and I've also heard Him call my name.

Because I hear God easily, I was convinced that was the only of my five senses with which I could communicate with God. I didn't believe I could see things in the Spirit, so I used to say, "I can hear God speak to me, but I can't see things with my spiritual eyes."

The Lord told me to stop saying I could not see in the Spirit because He wanted to enable me to do so. And guess what? I am now seeing things in the Spirit. Now, He's speaking to me about another area where He wants to bless me, and that is wisdom.

I used to say I didn't have much wisdom, at least not like my husband does. Jeff has incredible wisdom, which I've come to rely on. Now, I no longer say I don't have wisdom, because God is wanting to give me this gift also. He wants to give us wisdom both for ourselves and so we can share it with others.

There are two men mentioned in today's scripture readings who excelled in wisdom. One because he asked for wisdom and the other was stated as already having it.

"Give me an understanding heart so that I can govern your people well and know the difference between right and wrong."
— Solomon's prayer, 1 Kings 3:9

And it was said of Stephen in Acts 6:10 "None of them could stand against the wisdom and the Spirit with which Stephen spoke."

An "understanding heart" is defined as a heart that can "hear, understand and obey." Solomon was asking to hear God's voice, to understand what was meant and be given the ability to obey Him. Solomon knew this gift would serve him well as he ruled Israel and Judah. Solomon was known as the wisest man who ever lived; no one surpassed him in the wisdom God gifted him.

Today, I'm asking God to give me the same gift of wisdom Solomon asked for. I am certain that just like God gave me hearing, then seeing, He has brought me to understand the next gift that He wants me to have is wisdom.

And wisdom is not just for me.
James 1:5 NLT says,

"If you need wisdom, ask our generous God,
and he will give it to you. He will not rebuke you for asking."

# Day 160

## Children are a Blessing

1 Kings 5-6 / Acts 7:1-29 / Psalm 127 / Proverbs 16:28-30

What is the best gift you've ever received? You know that one gift that you had hoped for all year, or for many years. You dreamed of it, maybe you even saved up your money to buy it yourself. Maybe it's hard to narrow it down to just one gift, especially if you've been on earth awhile.

But there is one gift that outweighs many, and that is the gift of children. Whether you have children personally, or you delight in the children of others, Psalm 127:3 says,

> "Children are a gift from the LORD;
> they are a reward from Him."

I want to focus on the word "gift" in this verse. Over the years, as one who was raised in the church, it was with hushed shameful tones that a child out of wedlock was announced. This post is not to minimize the sin of sex outside of marriage. Rather I want to talk about the child.

Children are a gift no matter how they come about. Outside marriage, outside ideal circumstances, or even through means not wished for. Not everyone wants children, so it has been surprising to some to have to catch up to the fact of being pregnant. Some have even sought to abort the life, or to give the baby away to adoptive parents. Neither am I here to debate the morality of these choices, though I am solidly pro-life.

Again, may I say, no matter how a child is conceived, that child is a gift. And that child is innocent in his or her conception. That child is to be protected, provided for, loved, nurtured, and taught. That would be the ideal blessing for this little one. I'm thankful my parents wanted me and raised me in love.

Children are a gift from the LORD. The King James Version says children are a heritage. "Heritage" is defined as "property, inheritance, something inherited."

I've often said that my life's greatest work was in producing, loving, teaching and training our three children. And I still believe that. I have done and will do some beautiful things in my life, but to have a large part in mentoring three humans to be good people who love God and others is an accomplishment of a lifetime. And I believe they have each turned out to be amazing people!

If I inherited nothing else from God, I would be blessed with my family. I'm a firm believer that people are the only rewards and inheritance that are eternal. We can't take our homes or possessions with us when we leave earth; only the people whose lives we've impacted will matter when we're gone.

The next time you see a momma who's pregnant or has littles, please say a prayer of blessing for her. She's working so hard and even though she may be stressed at times, she is probably aware of the beauty of her life because of the sweet little ones God has given her.

Also, if you have an opportunity to impact a momma who is struggling with what to do about being pregnant, support and encourage her, and see what you can do to be part of the solution to her situation.

We are blessed so we can be a blessing. Seek to be a blessing to a child in your life this week!

# Day 161

## The Romans Road

1 Kings 7 / Acts 7:30-50 / Psalm 128 / Proverbs 16:31-33

Where are my people who love to research history, especially your family history? I am fascinated by family history and ancestry. I'm currently mired down in the kings of England heading back toward Scotland, Ireland and on into the era when the Biblical rulers merged their line with Ireland. That part of history is hard to find solid proof of because anything that would have been written down is scarce. Also, a lot of histories were told orally in ancient times.

That's why I'm fascinated with Stephen's telling of the history of Israel from the patriarchs to his current day. As I read, I wondered both how Stephen remembers all this history in such detail (I'm sure it was common for the oral histories to be rehearsed many times over someone's lifetime), and how the Jewish leaders are patient in listening to the account when this is supposed to be Stephen's defense for the false accusations against him.

They are, however, listening to every word. Since I've read the story before, I know what's coming. Stephen will tell the Jewish leaders how they crucified the Messiah, they will become angry, and Stephen will be stoned. But in the meanwhile, anyone who is listening is hearing an accurate account of the history that has led up to this point, though a very abbreviated one.

What about you? Are you confident of both your ancestral and more importantly your spiritual history? Could you tell the stories of the patriarchs, how the Messiah came, etc.? I'm sure the answers to this question will vary as each of us will be interested to different degrees in the details.

Whether you're a history nerd, or one who knows just enough details to know where you were born, there is one story which matters above every other. That is the history of the coming of Jesus Christ, first as a baby, and next as a King who will rule all things. If someone asked you to explain to them the Gospel of Salvation, could you?

If you're unsure, let me give you some scriptures that will help you get started. When I was a child, we shared Jesus with others using what was called "The Romans Road" to salvation. It's been so long since I've seen or used this that I am also having to look it up to share with you!

Romans 3:10 – No one is perfect
Romans 3:23 – Everyone sins
Romans 6:23 – Sin is death, but Jesus is life
Romans 5:8 – Christ took our sins
Romans 10:9 – Confess and believe to be saved
Romans 8:1 – People in Christ will be free
Jesus Saves!

Now you have a simple tool to walk someone toward salvation if you need it. Another amazing tool is to share your own personal story of experience with Jesus Christ. Practice your history, share it as often as you can and be a blessing to those you love, helping them know the One who loves us most!

# Day 162

## The Love of God

1 Kings 8 / Acts 7:51-8:13 / Psalm 129 / Proverbs 17:1

I love a good celebration, as I'm sure you do! I mean who doesn't love a good party with good food and presents! I love presents. I make lists, I dream, I look things up online and then I usually come back to reality and trim my list to the things I really need and will make good use of.

At this point in life, I don't need much. The house is already furnished and decorated, and I'm not one to spend more money every few years to redecorate.

Speaking of a good celebration, as I read the account of the dedication of the temple Solomon had built in 1 Kings 8, I imagined the immense celebration they had. Everything from speeches, prayers, overflowing sacrifices as was the custom of the day, to the glory of God filling the temple so that the priests could not do their job. That is something I'd love to experience!

And can you imagine the beauty of that temple? I would love to have seen that building in person after having read the detailed description. I bet it was beyond comparison with anything we've seen today. But beyond the beauty, beyond the celebration which lasted fourteen days, I'm struck by Solomon's prayer. This is a man who knows God. As I read the prayer, it was obvious that Solomon understood God's love and mercy during the shortcomings of the people of Israel.

Here are two parts of that prayer:

"You keep your covenant and show unfailing love to all who walk
before you in wholehearted devotion."
—1 Kings 8:23 b

"May you hear the humble and earnest requests from me and your
people Israel when we pray toward this place. Yes, hear us from
Heaven where you live, and when you hear, forgive."
—1 Kings 8:30

It's evident from Solomon's prayer that he understood God's
fathering nature, along with His heart to love His people and forgive
them. These are confident prayers from a man who knows his God.
Solomon is not cowering in fear, approaching God with an expectation of being punished.

Solomon is asking God to continue to show mercy to him and
God's people. And as we continue to read the Old Testament, we'll
see God's mercy and love repeatedly. Yes, God's people will worship
idols, leave Him behind, ignore Him, forget Him, and do evil and
terrible things. But time and time again, they will also be sorry for
their sins, remember God and ask for forgiveness.

And every time, God will hear them and show them mercy.
Sure, they'll still suffer from the choices they made, but even in the
suffering they will experience the kindness and goodness of God.

It's no different for us today. God is the same. He never leaves
us. He's always waiting for us to look to Him for help, to pray, to
ask for forgiveness, anything that would restore our connection with
Him. He's not the one who breaks connection; we are. He's never angry when we turn back and apologize for having ignored Him. He's
always ready with a smile, forgiveness and His immeasurable love.

# Day 163

## I'm a Bible Hugger

1 Kings 9-10 / Acts 8:14-40 / Psalm 130 / Proverbs 17:2-3

As a woman who continues to heal from and deal with trust issues, I appreciate when I find someone whose word I can count on. Obviously, it takes time to get to know a person and to determine whether their words match their actions. That is how I learn to trust someone. Please don't tell me one thing and do another; I will have lost respect for you already.

There is One whose words I have come to trust, rely on and put my hope in over my lifetime and that is God's Words. I love His written words of history in the Bible. I love the words He speaks to my heart, and I love that Jesus is referred to as The Word of God. I love that the Word is a Person. And this is what makes God's Word different from any other words I will ever read, hear or speak.

God's words have power behind them. It says in Hebrews 4:12,

"For the Word of God is alive and powerful.
It is sharper than the sharpest two-edged sword,
cutting between soul and spirit, between joint and marrow.
It exposes our innermost thoughts and desires."

James 1:22-24 says this, "But don't just listen to God's word. You must do what it says. Otherwise, you are only fooling yourselves. For if you listen to the word and don't obey, it is like glancing at your face in a mirror. You see yourself, walk away, and forget what you look like."

The truth contained in the words and history of the Bible are the body of beliefs after which I have chosen to pattern my life. I investigate the lives of the men and women there. I read their accounts and experiences. I realize they are speaking of a heavenly realm, from which I believe we came. Because we are of God's Spirit, we love Him, and we love what He speaks!

In today's reading I was comforted by Psalm 130:5 which reads,

> "I am counting on the LORD;
> yes, I am counting on Him.
> I have put my hope in His word."

For me, to know, read, follow and trust His words is to know, read, follow and trust Him. I learn Who He is, and I have a better idea of how He expects me to live as I read the inspired words of the writers of scripture.

I love God's Word, the Bible, so much that I've been known to slide it under my pillow or to hug it. And when I'm doing that, I'm not hugging a book; I'm hugging the One who inspired the book!

# Day 164

## Are You a Jesus Follower?

1 Kings 11:1-12:19 / Acts 9:1-25 / Psalm 131 / Proverbs 17:4-5

What we call ourselves, how we're named, or the groups to which we belong and with which we identify, is a big deal. Our names speak of identity and destiny. The groups with whom we align ourselves speak about our belief systems. You know the old saying, "You're known by the company you keep." My question to you is, "How are you known?"

How would you be identified? For me, I have many titles or identities. First, I'm Maria, and I talked about the meaning of my name in my devotional book based on a word for each week. I'm a daughter, a wife, a mom, a Gigi, and many more things.

I'm also a Christian, a Christ-follower, a Jesus-girl, and there are many more ways to say that. That's why I'm fascinated by Luke mentioning in the book of Acts that Saul was persecuting and arresting "any followers of the Way." In my research, I couldn't find a definitive answer as to why Jesus followers were called "The Way."

It is true that they were a sect, or a smaller group who had broken away from the traditional teachings of the larger group. Perhaps the religious leaders meant to insult those who were part of this group, but I happen to like the term. Why? Because in John 14:6 Jesus Himself said, "I am the way, the truth and the life." If Jesus called Himself "the Way," I'm good with His followers choosing to adopt that title.

After Saul's conversion and subsequent name change to Paul, he speaks in several verses throughout the book of Acts about how he used to persecute the followers of The Way. But he also began to identify himself as one of those followers. That's a real change of tune!

I personally prefer to call myself a follower of Jesus. The name "Christian" has unfortunately gotten a bad reputation because of the behavior of some. Christians should be like Christ in the earth, a representation of Him to everyone we meet. Sadly, our mistakes have a way of following us around.

No matter how you refer to yourself in relation to your faith in Christ, I pray your representation of Him is one that models His life on earth. He loved everyone He met. He hung out with those no one else would. And He changed lives everywhere He went!

May we go and do the same!

# Day 165

## *Four Lights in My Life*

1 Kings 12:20-13:34 / Acts 9:26-43 / Psalm 132 / Proverbs 17:6

Today, I want to talk to my readers who are grandparents. I've said this many times since my first grand-girl Heritage was born in November 2018, people who talked about how amazing it is to be grandparents way undersold the amazing, beautiful gift grandchildren are! Heritage, Oliver, Sophia and Psalm are lights in my life in such an incredible way. Yes, I adore my three children, but there is something so different about the joys of being a grandparent. What has me thinking about this, apart from the obvious admiration and love I hold for my "little people"?

Proverbs 17:6 reads,

> "Grandchildren are the crowning glory
> of the aged, parents are the pride of their children."

I will talk about both aspects in this entry because our family has been blessed coming and going with the relationships we've worked so hard to build!

Sadly, not everyone is blessed to have a good relationship with their grandchildren, children, or parents. If you have difficulty in any of these relationships, I'm so very sorry. I've experienced my own difficulties, but have worked hard to heal my soul and seek forgiveness for the sins of my ancestors, so that those who come after me have the opportunity to build on a more solid foundation.

That doesn't mean hard things don't happen. Health challenges, poor decisions, abuse, neglect and a thousand other things are always working against families and their desires to live in love.

That's why we must determine to work through the relationship issues now. Some things are out of our control, but we can forgive. We can be kind. We can treat someone other than the way they have treated us. This is not an easy choice, but I believe it's a necessary one if we want to live a peace-filled, and free life.

What about parents being the pride of their children? If you have great parents, you are blessed! No parent is perfect because they are working through their own past hurts and pain. To the degree they work through the past is the degree they will relate well to you. Guess what that means?

To the degree we work through our past hurts is the degree to which we can enjoy the relationships we have with our children. We are permitted to pass down blessings to our children and grandchildren instead of curses. But it takes someone being willing to stand up and say, "No more!"

That's not easy, but it's necessary! Someone must choose to be a sentinel for their generation and family. What is a sentinel? A sentinel is a soldier standing guard, or keeping watch, at a point of passage, such as a gate. We have a choice to either stand guard, not allowing things of the past to move forward in our lives, or to allow all kinds of destruction to get past us.

I am not allowing evil to get past me, at least as far as I'm aware. I can't know everything, but I can be alert, listening to Holy Spirit and guarding what is passed from me to those I love.

So, before you get old do your heart and soul work. I promise you do not want to be a crabby old man or woman and all because you refused to forgive and let go of stuff in the past. It's your choice to be a crabby old person or an old person that everyone loves to spend time with.

Even if you're young, please listen to what I'm saying. Take care of the business of your heart today. You will thank me when you're old. Well, I'll be in Heaven jumping clouds by then, but you'll still think fondly of my words and be glad you listened!

# Day 166

## Harmony in Unity

1 Kings 14:1-15:24 / Acts 10:1-23 / Psalm 133 / Proverbs 17:7-8

Unity in diversity, or different personalities coming together to produce strength as a community. Harmony in music comes when an orchestra plays a composition that sounds as if one voice is speaking. Just as an FYI, symphonies bring me to tears. Colors blended to make a new color create a work of art making one's heart race with the sight of the beauty. What do all these have in common? In each case, there are differing pieces being brought together to produce something that a single element cannot produce alone.

The benefits of community and unity are many. One benefit is that you can accomplish much more when connected with others who are like-minded and on a similar mission as you are. When you're weak, another is strong. When you're strong, another needs your help.

Psalm 133 from The Message reads this way, "How wonderful, how beautiful, when brothers and sisters get along! It's like costly anointing oil flowing down head and beard, flowing down Aaron's beard, flowing down the collar of his priestly robes. It's like the dew on Mount Hermon flowing down the slopes of Zion. Yes, that's where God commands the blessing, ordains eternal life."

This beautiful picture of unity is easy to read about, and it was probably easy for the author to write, but as we're all aware, it's much more difficult and challenging to live in unity or in oneness as Jesus prayed in John 17 that we would! Whether we are speaking about our birth family, our family by marriage, our church family, or our friends, to expect that we will always get along with each other is not realistic.

No two of us are created alike. Even twins have different personalities, along with likes, dislikes, gifts, talents, etc. Guess what that means? You're going to have to learn to love someone who is different from you. They will look different, act different, and like different things.

Differences will exist in the way they were raised, the types of food they like, the experiences they've had so far in life, the color of their skin, eyes and hair, and the abilities they have mentally, physically and emotionally. We could go on for hours with this list! Like the director of one of my favorite series *The Chosen* has said, "Get used to different!"

What am I to do when someone doesn't like something I like? I have a few choices. I can get upset and angry, and distance myself from them, or I can celebrate the difference. I can choose to learn from them, or I can shut them off. I hope you choose to learn from those who are different. I believe we can learn something from every person we meet if we're humble enough to admit we don't know everything.

I've seen hesitancy to accept differences, especially in a church setting. I mean, have you ever wondered why we have so many different denominations? On a practical level, the entire body of Christ could not come together in one place because there would be no room. But on a spiritual level, every person who has been born into the family of God through Jesus Christ is my brother or sister.

I understand that some people are mean, or dangerous, and I'm not advocating we become intimate with those who would harm us. But apart from harm to our physical, emotional or spiritual being, we have such an opportunity to learn, grow and become richer by choosing to be in relationship with others who want to become like Jesus.

So, find your people. Forgive the ones who have hurt you. Walk away from the ones who are truly harmful. Agree to disagree when topics are trivial. But please do not isolate yourself from people who are safe, good, and will bring great treasure into your life. Unity and oneness are achieved when we lay aside the differences that don't matter to extend our hearts to another human being, a human who is as imperfect as we are.

I could probably write for another page, but I want to keep this entry relatively short as usual. I understand that you've been hurt by people, by institutions, even by those who say they love Jesus. I have also been hurt. And I've shared my stories of forgiveness and choosing to move forward. I've chosen to trust again, to build again and to allow others in again.

Would you agree to do that with me? Let's go for unity, harmony, oneness, a beautiful orchestration or work of art. I know it's possible!

# Day 167

## Why Water Baptism?

1 Kings 15:25-17:24 / Acts 10:24-48 / Psalm 134 / Proverbs 17:9-11

Our house church, Bethesda Springs House of Mercy and Grace, recently decided to study about baptisms. We studied baptism in water, baptism into the body of Christ, baptism of fire, and baptism in the Holy Spirit. We started with water baptism. For me, this conversation was important because I've been having my foundational beliefs wrecked as I move away from the doctrines of men, being sure what I believe lines up with scripture.

Before I was born again, I clearly heard God tell me I needed to be saved, so I obeyed what I was hearing. I was water baptized at the age of seven in the James River near Hampton, Virginia. I don't remember God speaking to me about this baptism. I think I was water baptized because that's what was expected. I was baptized by Holy Spirit for the first time at the age of 11. I may talk more about that in a later entry.

As I mentioned, my foundation is being wrecked and rebuilt. Many of the teachings I've heard and received were laced with legalism, however the Lord is rebuilding me with a foundation of His grace and love. It's painful to have your foundation jack-hammered and redone!

As we studied baptisms, I found myself wrestling about water baptism. Why do we need to be water baptized? What does water baptism gain for us, other than the fact of obeying Jesus's example?

It's not wrong for us to ask the "why" questions. We must know why we believe what we believe and why we do what we do. So, when

I read about Cornelius and his family receiving faith in Christ, along with Holy Spirit falling on them, and when I read that orders were given for them all to be baptized in the name of Jesus Christ, reading these events caused me to want to better understand baptisms.

Scripture establishes that salvation and water baptism are separate experiences, and that water baptism is an outward expression of what has happened inwardly when we receive salvation by faith through grace. (See Acts 10:40-48)

This scripture, along with many others, shows that salvation is received first, apart from water baptism. Water baptism is not necessary for salvation. So, why be water baptized?

The example in scripture is that most who received salvation followed their declaration of faith in Christ with an outward demonstration of that inward faith by being immersed in water. Who knows whether the verses that depict salvation apart from water baptism simply do not tell the rest of the story, or if some were not water baptized for various reasons. Not every detail of every event is written in the history of scripture.

The "why" of water baptism is answered this way:

Choosing to be baptized is our "first witness" to our inward change. When we have received Christ, we are made new creatures as it says in 1 Corinthians 5:17.

Romans 6:4-6 tells us,

"Therefore we have been buried with him by baptism into death, so that, just as Christ was raised from the dead by the glory of the Father, so we too might walk in newness of life. For if we have been united with him in a death like his, we will certainly be united with him in a resurrection like his. We know that our old self was crucified with him so that the body of sin might be destroyed, and we might no longer be enslaved to sin."

My conclusion in favor of water baptism is that if I have become a new creature, and if I now want to be like Christ, I want to follow Him in the path He walked which is the path of death, burial, and resurrection to new life. By being immersed through water baptism, I am stating that I want my old nature dead and buried, and I want to be raised to my new nature in Jesus Christ.

I'm one who loves drawing lines in the sand so to speak. I have a feeling that in the Spirit world a line is drawn in the sand when we make a public profession of faith by submitting to water baptism. Why would I quietly receive Christ, then hide the beautiful gift I've been given? I would only hide the gift if I'm ashamed of it, and I am not ashamed of the Gospel of Jesus Christ because it is the power of God for salvation. (from Romans 1:16)

If you have not been water baptized, please consider doing so. Or if you have been water baptized and you are feeling compelled to make a recommitment, please also do that!

# Day 168

## What Do I Do with Mean People?

1 Kings 18 / Acts 11 / Psalm 135 / Proverbs 17:12-13

Have you ever worked hard to be nice to someone who is mean? I'm sure you'd much rather be mean back. I'll be honest in saying my first thoughts are sometimes to lash out or get back at them for what they did. We've talked a lot about forgiveness this year, and that's because I've needed to do a lot of forgiving.

When we're kind to people, we expect they will be kind in return. When people are unkind, we may try at first to be kind, thinking that maybe they've had a bad day, or they are going through a rough time. I think that's the case most of the time when someone is being unkind. We don't know the things that are happening in people's lives that cause them to be rude, hateful, or just plain mean.

Proverbs 17:13 is scary when thinking about the concept of good versus evil.

"If you repay good with evil, evil will never leave your house."

Let's look at the definition of the words "good" and "evil" to get a better understanding. We want to avoid the potential for evil never leaving our house!

The word "good" is defined as "prosperity, happiness, good things, moral good, or bounty." Basically, anything we have that would be a blessing when given to another person. That could be our time, love, belongings, etc.

The word "evil" is defined as "giving pain, misery, or unhappiness vicious in disposition, ethically wicked." I believe most people are good at heart, so it's rare to find someone who is truly evil and determined to harm us.

I don't know if you've ever had anyone respond with evil when you were good to them. It's likely that at least some of us have experienced this. How did you respond? Even more, how should we respond?

First and always, we must forgive them. Second, we must determine if that person is allowed to remain in our close circle, even if they are family. Remember, we have permission to create distance for our own safety and good.

Sometimes it's difficult or even impossible to remove ourselves from being around someone who is evil. That's a harder scenario. The only solution there is to pray that God would deliver you from the situation, and that He would protect you until deliverance comes.

My next question is, "Does it seem fair that someone would have evil 'never leave his house?'" NEVER leave? In these cases, I'm glad I'm not God and not responsible for making the decisions on the law of reaping what we've sown. The level of our reaping what we've sown is subject to God's love and mercy, as well as our repentance.

We can pray for the evil person, hoping they repent and find Jesus. Beyond that, we need to mind our own hearts and be sure we're not repaying anyone evil for the good they have done for us.

The bottom line is, we must forgive all those who wrong us. And I do mean all, because remember that forgiveness is for your sake, whether the other person ever changes or not. If someone is being mean or evil to you, make your best attempt to appeal to them first; maybe they are not aware. If they won't hear you, take another person along with you and make another attempt. (read Matthew 18:15)

Depending on the situation, you may want to distance yourself until they see what they are doing to you. Sometimes the distance is enough to alert the mean person about their inappropriate behavior.

I pray you can work through the relationship issues you are facing. Breaches in relationships are tougher than many other things we must deal with.

# Day 169

## His Faithful Love Endures Forever

1 Kings 19 / Acts 12:1-23 / Psalm 136 / Proverbs 17:14-15

When you get into a fight with someone whether a family member, a friend, or an enemy, what is your first response, or your weapon of choice? Do you run? Do you yell, speak insults, or pout? Or do you lay down your weapons and attempt to diffuse the situation, so it won't escalate into an all-out war?

Everyone is different in how they handle arguments, or as Jeff and I call them, discussions. We don't raise our voices because we see no point. I wish I could say we didn't raise our voices when we were younger. But we've learned a lot since we got married in 1989.

In God's kingdom our weapons are exactly the opposite of what one would expect. Two people yelling at each other won't bring a solution. Neither will two people who are angry or fearful. We have the power of Holy Spirit inside us, allowing us to wage war differently from the world. But how do we do that?

In the kingdom of God, one of our weapons is love. So, instead of us showing anger or shouting insults, we can choose to speak with love. As I read Psalm 136 today, I was more aware of our strong weapon called love. Every other line in the Psalm, throughout the entire Psalm, is "His faithful love endures forever."

Since God operates in faithful love, we must do the same. Do you have someone being evil to you? Pray about how to show the love of Jesus. I realize I'm asking you to do something hard. God will ask us to be kind to and continue to pray for those who are our enemies.

Let's define "faithful love" so we can better understand what is required of us.

His faithful love, or His "mercy" as stated in the King James Version, is defined as:

> "kindness, goodness, favor, lovingkindness in
> condescending to the needs of His creatures.
> Specifically, this lovingkindness is shown in redemption
> from enemies and troubles."

God in His perfection always shows us love, regardless of our behavior, thoughts and responses to Him. If God always shows love, even to those who are enemies of His, we also ought to show love.

When we're angry, His faithful love endures forever. When we're sad, His faithful love endures forever. When we're grieving, His faithful love endures forever. When we're happy and content, His faithful love endures forever. No matter what we do or where we go His faithful love endures forever.

We have access to His love any time we need it both because we are His and because He lives inside us. So, the next time you're ready to shout, or stomp or get angry, maybe your prayer could be, "Lord, awaken my heart to the fact that Your love is always with me, and even within me because of Your Spirit. Remind me to turn to You when my emotions are out of control. I want to receive Your kindness both because I need it and because I want to give it away. Amen!"

# Day 170

## Why Do Evil People Get Away with Things?

1 Kings 20-21 / Acts 12:24-13:15 / Psalm 137 / Proverbs 17:16

We get irritated when people who treat other people with injustice still seem to prosper financially, relationally, etc. Sometimes, those who do horrible things to others seem to escape punishment. We know that evil won't be eradicated until this earth passes away, but it's frustrating to see bad people doing bad things and appearing to get away with it.

Although evil people may appear to get away with things, they will give an account before God for what they've done if they do not repent. What if you're the kind of person who would rather do good things, but bad things still happen to you? It seems like a terrible injustice, especially when there is a law set in place by God that we reap what we've sown.

Yes, we will reap what we've sown. Interestingly, there is no time frame placed upon the reaping. Some may reap immediately, some may take a short time, and some may take a long time. Some may not realize the error of their ways until they're standing before God and suddenly discover that because they are not in Christ, they are guilty of all they've done. This makes us thankful that no matter what comes our way, both good and evil, we are in Christ.

As I read today about Ahab and Jezebel, I had forgotten that God attempted to reveal Himself to Ahab by helping him defeat the king of Aram, not once but twice! God wasn't helping Ahab because he was a good man. Ahab and his wife were very evil, worshipping idols, along with all sorts of terrible things. But God, in His mercy, still attempted to prove Himself to this evil man. Of course, Ahab only partially obeyed God and his dynasty was destroyed in the time of his son's reign.

If evil will happen to good people and good will happen to evil people, why does it matter how we live while on earth? There's another scripture in Matthew 5:43-48 that informs how we are to behave considering both good and evil existing around us.

> "You have heard the law that says, 'Love your neighbor' and hate your enemy.' But I say, 'Love your enemies! Pray for those who persecute you!' In that way, you will be acting as true children of your Father in Heaven. For he gives his sunlight to both the evil and the good, and he sends rain on the just and the unjust alike. If you love only those who love you, what reward is there for that? Even corrupt tax collectors do that much. If you are kind only to your friends, how are you different from anyone else? Even pagans do that. But you are to be perfect, even as your Father in Heaven is perfect."

Why should we love our enemies? First, we will prove we belong to God and are His children. Second, there is a reward for treating our enemies with love. Third, by loving our enemies we are proving we are different from those who don't know God.

Finally, loving our enemies allows us to become "perfect." The Greek word for "perfect" is "teleios," and it's an adjective which means "mature, full-grown adult, wanting nothing necessary to completeness."

As a side note, "teleios" is a similar word to what Jesus said from the cross when He said, "It is finished." That Greek word was "teleo," and it is a verb which means "to bring to a close, to finish, to end."

Jesus finished His work on the cross; let's finish our work through Him by loving those who are unlovable.

# Day 171

## Speak Truth or Keep Quiet?

1 Kings 22 / Acts 13:16-41 / Psalm 138 / Proverbs 17:17-18

How difficult is it for you to speak the truth when everyone around you is doing otherwise? It's sometimes easier to avoid conflict and keep silent in the face of falsehoods, but if you've ever been in that situation, you know how the lies will eat at your soul until you speak up. Either that, or you'll avoid those people and situations due to not wanting to be confrontational.

I'll be honest, I've done some of all of these. I've avoided people, topics, and situations, but I've also spoken up when truth was being mangled. There are times when leaving people in their own deception is necessary because they may not be ready to hear the truth. There are also times when speaking up will allow someone to see the truth and gain freedom. We must discern which scenario we're in.

As I read in 1 Kings 22, I was fascinated by the story of the 400 prophets prophesying one thing to King Ahab, while the prophet Micaiah spoke only what he heard God say. Unfortunately, speaking the truth caused the prophet to be thrown into prison and given only bread and water until Ahab had returned safely from battle.

Of course, Ahab did not return because Micaiah had heard God correctly that Ahab was going to be killed in the battle. The 400 prophets were deceived by evil spirits and prophesying lies, telling Ahab to go into battle and that he would be victorious. In the end, the truth prevailed. I wonder what happened to the 400 false prophets. And hopefully Micaiah was released from prison.

We're not likely to be threatened with prison if we tell the truth, however, there is the potential that we'll be shunned or spoken ill of for our stance. If you knew the truth and you knew by speaking up you would be mocked, would you still speak the truth? That's a tough question.

However, it is something to consider. Let's decide now how we are going to respond in these situations. We will be more confident and bolder if we decide ahead of time we're going to stand up for the truth.

If you're able, it's also a good idea to take a friend with you when it's time to speak the truth. Your friend will help boost your courage and you're more likely to be bold. That whole "strength in numbers" thing is real!

Please give this topic about truth and boldness to speak some thought. Pray and ask God to help you be bold with truth, no matter what it may cost you. Pray to be filled with Holy Spirit because it is He who gives us boldness to be a witness for God's kingdom!

# Day 172

## *Let Jesus Remove Your Thorns*

2 Kings 1-2 / Acts 13:42-14:7 / Psalm 139 / Proverbs 17:19-21

Let's have a little fun today. Let's share our deepest darkest secrets with one another. You go first! No? I don't understand why you don't want me to know your dirt, your junk, your hidden issues. Hmph.

I'm sure none of us wants everyone to know our secrets, much less our deepest and darkest. You know, the things you think about that you hope no one ever finds out. Like that you wish so and so would choke on a chicken bone, or that person who wronged you would get what's coming to her. Or that you wish you had your neighbor's beautiful house or boat.

We want to be known as kind, good people who would never hurt anyone, but the truth is there are times when our hearts are just plain evil.

Jeremiah 17:9 says

"The heart is deceitful above all things and beyond cure.
Who can understand it? "

I think there are times when we don't even realize the hidden things that are in our hearts. Maybe we've been hurt or rejected so we harbor those things, and it causes our hearts to be impure. All of us need emotional healing. And God is ready and waiting to provide that.

So, when we read verses like Psalm 139:23-24, we don't need to get anxious and try to hide because God wants to heal us if we'll let Him. Let's read these two verses in The Passion Translation.

"God, I invite your searching gaze into my heart. Examine me through and through; find out everything that may be hidden within me. Put me to the test and sift through all my anxious cares. See if there is any path of pain I'm walking on, and lead me back to your glorious, everlasting way — the path that brings me back to you."

Some may think this is an invitation to a "this is everything you've done wrong" session, but if you'll read carefully, it's God's way of finding the pain inside and bringing healing where it's needed, including healing in our relationship with Him.

I love the part of those verses that reads, "See if there is any path of pain I'm walking on." That sounds like a plea for help! These verses remind me of the fairy tale I heard as a child. It's the story of Androcles and the Lion. Here's one account of the story.

"Androcles was a runaway slave of a former Roman consul administering a part of Africa. He took shelter in a cave, which turned out to be the den of a wounded lion, from whose paw he removed a large thorn. In gratitude, the lion became tame towards him and henceforward shared his catch with the slave.

"After three years, Androcles craved a return to civilization but was soon imprisoned as a fugitive slave and sent to Rome. There he was condemned to be devoured by wild animals in the Circus Maximus in the presence of an emperor who was named in the account as Gaius Caesar, presumably Caligula.

"The most imposing of the beasts turned out to be the same lion, which again displayed its affection toward Androcles. After questioning him, the emperor pardoned the slave in recognition of this testimony to the power of friendship, and he was left in possession of the lion."

If we liken ourselves to the lion, and God is likened to Androcles, you will see that God in His mercy only wants to show His great love to us by removing the things from our lives that are harming us. Once God has healed and comforted us, we are grateful to Him for the rest of our days.

# Day 173

## Yes, I am My Brother's Keeper

2 Kings 3:1-4:17 / Acts 14:8-28 / Psalm 140 / Proverbs 17:22

The Church, also known as Jesus' bride, the body of Christ, or Jesus followers, has an awesome responsibility to one another. When you first said "yes" to Jesus calling your name and wanting to forgive and heal you, you may not have realized you were becoming part of a large, global family. You may not have been aware that you were gaining mothers, fathers, brothers, and sisters. These are now your blood relatives because of what Jesus Christ did on the cross.

We are thankful for our birth family (if we're blessed to have them as a healthy part of our lives) and how we fit into that dynamic. But being aware of how we fit into the body of Christ is a little more complex. The complexity comes when we realize we have a responsibility to love and encourage those who are part of this Christ family. It is our role to speak life, health, and peace over this new family.

Sadly, some parts of Jesus's body are not aware of this task of strengthening others and they inadvertently tear the body apart, damaging and wounding those Christ loves. We all have times when we hurt others. The important part to remember is that once you're aware you've hurt another, ask for his forgiveness. It takes humility to be part of this large family because we will not always get it right.

As I read Acts 14:22, I was drawn to the portion that reads,

> "They strengthened the believers. They encouraged them to continue in the faith, reminding them that we must suffer many hardships to enter the Kingdom of God."

Paul and Barnabas are strengthening others, obeying what Jesus taught them about making disciples. And those who are receiving strength are the new believers in each town Paul and Barnabas have visited.

What does it look like to strengthen someone? Or to encourage someone to continue in the faith? We're going to study this further because I believe this is the role of every believer. We must always seek to strengthen and encourage those in our Jesus family!

The word "strengthen" is defined as "to establish, render more firm or confirm." This definition reminds me about the importance of building a strong foundation. In the Christian journey, truth is the foundation upon which we build. So, let's call truth the foundation of a person's "building."

What are the truths that we must use as our foundation? These are the things spoken of in "The Apostle's Creed," which I have shared with you before. In short, our foundation is built upon Jesus Christ and everything He did by coming to earth.

The word "encourage" is defined as "to call to one's side, to comfort, to speak to, instruct, teach." Encouragement is now being built upon the foundation of truth. Our building has begun to take shape!

Our accepting of truth is more than someone telling us what to do and us following through. We have the privilege of coming alongside one another to give understanding, to lift each other up when we are weak, and to cheer each other on toward great success. It is important that we invest in one another's lives because then we all become who God has called us to be.

Therefore, when I enter the family of God, it is no longer a matter of looking out for myself only. Yes, I must learn to feed myself, but I must also learn to feed others with what I've been given.

Philippians 2:4 states,

> "Don't look out only for your own interests,
> but take an interest in others, too."

In the world, we are interested only in how we can get ahead. In the body of Christ, it is our honor to monitor our own growth but also to encourage the growth of our God-family.

If my sister or brother is not growing, I must ask God what I can do to help. Sometimes I am asked to pray, sometimes to speak, and sometimes to walk with them. Whatever my role in the growth of another, it's a blessing to be part of that one knowing Jesus more!

# Day 174

## God is a Multiplier

2 Kings 4:18-5:27 / Acts 15:1-35 / Psalm 141 / Proverbs 17:23

Some prefer to read the Old Testament, and some prefer the New Testament, but I'm one who loves both! Some say the God of the Old Testament is angry and short-tempered, while the God of the New Testament is kind, and full of grace. But if God is always the same, which is the truth?

Hebrews 13:8 tells us this,

"Jesus Christ is the same yesterday, today and forever."

God does not change. Yes, He is angry at sin. And yes, He is full of grace toward those who repent. He is the same in all of scripture. In today's reading, I found a story I had missed when I've read these passages before.

You may remember that Jesus did many miracles in the Gospels (Matthew, Mark, Luke and John) where He took a small amount of food and multiplied it to feed thousands of people. He also made wine at a wedding. Now that would have been fun to witness!

However, I had not seen the story where God multiplied food in the Old Testament, but it's right there plain as day. 2 Kings 4:42-44 is a short story, but it's an account where ten loaves of barley bread were able to feed 100 people with bread left over.

In this case, it is the prophet Elisha who confidently led the scenario according to what the LORD had promised. I don't know whether we've ever had a food miracle. There have certainly been times when it looked as if we wouldn't have enough to feed everyone. There have been times when we've run out, as well as times when we've had more than enough. Maybe I should start paying attention so I don't accidentally miss my own miracle!

Up until today, I thought God only multiplied food in the New Testament, but I can see that I was mistaken. God, the God who does not change, was able to provide multiplication of resources throughout all of scripture. And that tells me He can still do the same today.

God also provided food while the children of Israel were wandering around in the desert. He gave them manna (a sweet flaky substance), and at one point He gave them quail. He provided water on several occasions when none could be found. God loves to provide for His people.

So, whether you need food, clothing, shelter, healing or whatever, God can provide for what you need. Sometimes we forget to ask Him for things that we see as mundane, but I believe He enjoys the small as well as the large miracles.

What do you need today? I think you should ask Him to provide for you. When He does, pay close attention and share the story with someone! Or if He has already provided something, I hope you can rejoice in the memory of that.

God will also provide seed to those who sow. Are you a giver? God will give to you so you can give to others. As you give away what you have, God will provide more. You'll always have enough and so will those around you.

I've shared this truth with our daughter Abigail many times because she is one of the largest "sowers" I know. She gives and gives.

It's an incredible gift she has. And guess what! She always has more than enough for herself and those she loves.

So, after you've asked God to provide, find someone to whom you may give, and give with all your heart, knowing that God will provide for your needs.

# Day 175

## A Gathering of Jesus Followers

2 Kings 6-7 / Acts 15:36-16:15 / Psalm 142 / Proverbs 17:24-25

There are many perspectives on what a church gathering should look like. Some believe the group must meet in a certain building. Some believe there must be certain elements included for the gathering to be a true Christian service. Some believe anywhere the body of Christ gathers is to be considered the Church.

It doesn't matter what you believe about the forms we observe. Whether meeting inside a building or a home. Whether singing from a hymnal or singing the latest songs on the radio. Whether reading scripture passages only or taking the time to study the Bible in depth. Whether altar calls, communion, or many other things that might be included. Any time Christians gather and honor the name of Christ, His presence is there, and "church" has been experienced.

Some prefer traditional organ music with hymns, some enjoy a guitar and what we used to call scripture choruses. Some want a carefully laid out order of service, and some prefer a structure that allows Holy Spirit to direct within a certain framework.

That's why I found it interesting that on the Sabbath Paul and Silas were not in the synagogue, but rather they went outside the city to a riverbank where they expected other believers would be gathered to pray. They were in the large city of Philippi, so I would guess there was a synagogue in which to meet. The text doesn't tell us why they chose to meet in a non-traditional place. Maybe they were looking for those not normally found in the traditional setting.

No matter the reason for the change in the usual routine of

meeting in the synagogue, Paul and Silas found themselves talking with a woman named Lydia. She was a merchant of expensive purple cloth, so she was likely wealthy. She also worshiped God. She easily received the message preached because the Lord opened her heart to the truth. And God did all that on a riverbank, outside the city.

Scripture says Lydia and her household were baptized, so evidently, they were also ready to hear the message of truth brought to them. I'm fascinated by the concept of someone, along with their household, being baptized. As I studied, I found varied opinions on the topic.

Since it would be inappropriate to force Christianity upon someone who was not ready, I don't believe Lydia compelled her household to be baptized. One of two things likely happened. Either her family members were with her, heard the message, believed, and were baptized. Or she shared the message with them when she returned home, they believed, and wanted to be baptized.

If you have received Christ and been baptized, and your household did not follow you in your faith, there is still hope and time. I wish it were as simple as every member believing together, but that does not always happen. I will encourage you not to give up praying and believing for the salvation of your family members.

They have seen your journey and heard your testimony. I believe faith has already been planted within their hearts and that at the right time, God will cause them to respond to His truth and love.

So, whether in a traditional or non-traditional setting. Whether with an organ, a guitar or a whole band. Whether communion is observed or not. Jesus Christ is well able to meet His people wherever they gather, and He can bring growth and change to them by His Word and Spirit.

# Day 176

## *My Fear Doesn't Stand a Chance*

2 Kings 8:1-9:13 / Acts 16:16-40 / Psalm 143 / Proverbs 17:26

If you've ever struggled with depression, you know how hopeless and helpless this state of mind can make you feel. If you have not struggled with depression, you may not understand that one cannot simply "help themselves" out of it. If someone is trapped here, they need help from the Lord and from those around them who are equipped to help.

I have had seasons of depression and seasons where I felt I've overcome it. When it was at its worst, I felt there was nothing I could do to escape. This was the time when I knew deep inside me God was still there, so I turned my worship music up louder to drown out the darkness and to bring hope to my burdened soul.

I wish I could say I was suddenly delivered, or that the depression left and never returned. Thankfully, I'm doing well today. Also, thankfully I've had the experience of walking through depression because now I'm able to have compassion for and walk with those who are still trying to get free.

I found a powerful key to help as we walk toward freedom. It's in Psalm 143:7-12 from our reading today. Here's the text for you to read again.

"Come quickly, Lord, and answer me, for my depression deepens. Don't turn away from me, or I will die. Let me hear of your unfailing love each morning, for I am trusting you. Show me where to walk, for I give myself to you. Rescue me from my enemies, Lord; I run to you to hide me. Teach me to do your will, for you are my God. May your gracious Spirit lead me forward on a firm footing. For the glory of your name, O Lord, preserve my life. Because of your faithfulness, bring me out of this distress. In your unfailing love, silence all my enemies and destroy all my foes, for I am your servant."

What is the powerful key that unlocks freedom found hiding in this verse? These words are our powerful key: "Let me hear of your unfailing love each morning, for I am trusting You."

When depression is kicking your butt, you are desperate to hear the truth that will pull you out of the darkness. And it is the unfailing love of God that is powerful enough to pull you out. Even when I couldn't think straight, even when I was hopeless that life would ever change, I still knew deep in my heart that God was there and that He loved me.

I trusted Him. Since I was helpless, He had to show me what to do. I certainly couldn't put two thoughts together to figure that out for myself. So, I ran to Him to hide, knowing He would protect me in my weakness. I looked to Him to lead me to a place where my feet could feel firmness again instead of the slippery, fearful place I had existed.

And of course, when we are down, when we are weak, when we see no hope and no way out, the enemy is gloating. But God sees that, and He rescues us!

While I can't say how long the depression may last for you, I can say that God is there, and He wants to lead you out to a firm place. He wants to heal and deliver you. He wants you to be free.

If you're struggling today or you have in the past, you understand what I'm saying. And I encourage you to look up because He sees you. Turn up your worship music and remember that He hears you. Bow your head in prayer because He knows how you feel. He will help you. He will be with you. He will not abandon you in this hard place.

245

# Day 177

## *You are a Mighty Warrior*

2 Kings 9:14-10:31 / Acts 17 / Psalm 144 / Proverbs 17:27-28

Who among my readers considers yourself to be a warrior in the Spirit? Today, I want to talk to you about your inheritance and your rights as a son or daughter of the King. I don't think most of us realize who we are in Christ. We are not simply humans existing here on earth. We are so much more, and we are meant to accomplish great and mighty things in God's Kingdom!

Why do I believe this? Because scripture tells us the truth of who we are in Christ. There is not enough time in this entry to lay out our entire inheritance, but wouldn't that be a fascinating study! It would likely take the rest of our lifetime to grasp. However, I will start with a portion from Psalm 144 and another from Psalm 8. Psalm 8 is something I was reading a few days ago apart from my regular reading.

"Praise the LORD, who is my rock. He trains my hands
for war and gives my fingers skill for battle. He is my loving ally
and my fortress, my tower of safety, my rescuer.
He is my shield, and I take refuge in Him.
He makes the nations submit to me."
— Psalm 144:1-2

"You gave them (us) charge of everything you made,
putting all things under their (our) authority."
— Psalm 8:6

These two sections from the Psalms give us a great peek into who we are and what God has given us. We have been given authority over all things God made. Did you know that? ALL things are under our authority; everything God created both in the natural realm and in the spirit realm.

But we don't wield this authority alone. Did you see in Psalm 144 that God is our "loving ally"? As I've read through the Old Testament this year, I've noticed that alliances were made before going to war. Most kings did not fight alone, but instead asked a neighboring king to align with them before they went into battle.

It is not different with us; except we have the King of the universe as our ally. That means victory is assured because scripture says in 1 Corinthians 15:27 about Jesus Christ, "God has put all things under His authority." And again, because we are in Christ, all things are also under our authority. Is this a double whammy? I think so!

Your ally is the King of the universe. Everything is under His authority. He has also given us authority over all things. So, why do we get our butts kicked at times? I think it's because we have forgotten to take our position of power in God's Spirit.

When Jesus was on the cross the last words He spoke were, "It is finished." He still had to go into hell and destroy the devil, taking away the keys to death, hell, and the grave. But I believe the minute Jesus breathed his last, the devil knew he had lost everything. The devil thought He was killing the King of the universe and that he would now have free reign. Not so.

Jesus went into enemy territory and annihilated the domain of satan. Since that victory is the foundation we build upon, we are now free to destroy every work the enemy attempts to bring against us. We can stand against every temptation, sickness, sorrow, etc. that satan throws at us. And make no mistake, these are the weapons the devil attempts to use against us. But they have no real power!

We are the ones who hold the power and authority over every evil thing because of what Jesus Christ has given us! I implore you to believe this, take hold of this, walk in this truth and see if your entire life doesn't shift. You will begin to walk in victory instead of defeat. Will things still irritate you? Yes, but you are armed to battle all things!

So, put on your armor (read Ephesians 6) and get to it! No sitting around. No whining and complaining. Take up your sword and shield mighty warrior and put the devil back in his place. He has no rights and no authority in your life.

# Day 178

*Let's be Like Jesus*

2 Kings 10:32-12:21 / Acts 18:1-22 / Psalm 145 / Proverbs 18:1

Have you ever known a short-tempered person? Or been that short-tempered person yourself? I've known some angry people both in my family and among those who have been friends. I'm very sensitive to angry people because someone close to me growing up had issues with anger. Then because of that person's modeled behavior, I became an angry person. Until the Lord had a little talk with me.

I don't remember when the anger started, but I remember it being an issue until about 1991 or so. I remember the general time because it was when my oldest was a little guy and he was the only child I had at the time. I had what we would today call "road rage" so I regularly yelled at drivers, telling them how "stupid" they were, etc.

On a certain day, someone cut me off in traffic and in my anger, I yelled out, "You dumb a**!" The Spirit of God immediately said to me, "You will never do that again." And something instantly shifted in my heart. I was so convicted, not only of my anger and bad language, but also because my little boy was seeing a behavior that I didn't want to pass on.

I wish I could say I never get angry now, but there are still times when I do. I have learned to quickly forgive the anger source and calm myself down before I also need forgiveness! When I read Psalm 145:8-9 today, I realized that if God is slow to get angry, He also expects us to be this way. Here's what those verses tell us.

"The LORD is merciful and compassionate, slow to get angry and filled with unfailing love. The LORD is good to everyone. He showers compassion on all his creation."

We need to ask God to increase our faith as the disciples did when faced with needing to always forgive. If the Lord is merciful, so must we be. If He is compassionate, so must we be. If He is slow to get angry, so must we be, and so on. We are all a work in progress and none of us does this perfectly. But hopefully we're growing to be more like Jesus daily.

That has been my hope and prayer for many years; to be changing and growing, and that my growth would be evident to those around me. Why? Because my growth brings honor to Jesus. This is not so I receive praise, although it is nice to hear that I've grown. Ultimately, this is so my life is a light in dark places and so others see Jesus Christ and are drawn to Him.

Anger, hatred, bitterness. All of these are the language of hell and not the language of Heaven. I want to "speak" the language of Heaven. That language begins with my thoughts, then travels to my heart and finally comes out of my mouth. So, if my mouth is running away without me, I better check my heart, then guard my thoughts.

This gives a whole new meaning to taking our thoughts captive and to guarding the wellspring of our hearts. (read 2 Corinthians 10:5 and Proverbs 4:23)

The more we grow, the more growth we will realize we still need. Let's be thankful to be covered under God's love, grace, mercy, and forgiveness, and His blood that cleanses us from all sin!

# Day 179

## Baptisms Continued

2 Kings 13-14 / Acts 18:23-19:12 / Psalm 146 / Proverbs 18:2-3

In a recent entry, I mentioned that we at Bethesda Springs house church had studied baptisms. I thought I knew all about baptism, but I found out that I had a lot of partial truths and that there is much to learn about these foundational pieces of our Christian faith.

Today, as I read Acts 19:1-6, my understanding was further expanded. I knew that John's baptism was one of repentance because it could not have been more until Messiah came. Jesus had to be crucified and raised again before salvation could be offered. So, when John was baptizing others, they were not being saved. Maybe it seems too simple to state that.

In these 6 verses, we're hearing about Apollos who came from Alexandria in Egypt. He was a gifted and accurate teacher of scripture who taught at Corinth. While Apollos was in Corinth, Paul traveled to Ephesus in Turkey and found several believers who lived there. When Paul asked them about having received the Holy Spirit, they said they had not, and that they had received only the baptism of John, which was repentance from their sins.

They did not yet know, possibly because they did not have the letters and scriptures that we have today, about the baptism that Jesus brought. But as soon as they heard, they were baptized in the name of the Lord Jesus, receiving salvation and water baptism.

It may have been they were not aware Messiah had come, and the salvation John spoke of was now available for them to receive.

Afterward, Paul laid his hands on them, the Holy Spirit came on them, and they spoke in other tongues and prophesied.

Now these believers have received the gift of repentance, the gift of salvation and the gift of the Holy Spirit. There is so much to experience in God and if you're like me, you don't want to miss any of it!

To clear up any possible confusion, let's look at the Greek word for "baptism."

The word "baptism" is "baptisma" in the Greek language and refers to "immersion" or "submersion."

The Strong's concordance says of John's baptism, "that purification rite by which men on confessing their sins were bound to spiritual reformation, obtained the pardon of their past sins and became qualified for the benefits of the Messiah's Kingdom soon to be set up."

The Strong's also says, "This was valid Christian baptism, as this was the only baptism the apostles received, and it is not recorded anywhere that they were ever rebaptized after Pentecost."

Further, "Of Christian baptism – a rite of immersion in water as commanded by Christ, by which one after confessing his sins and professing his faith in Christ, having been born again by the Holy Spirit unto a new life, identifies publicly with the fellowship of Christ and the church."

Not every detail of what happened is written in the body of scripture we have available. Maybe the apostles were baptized after Jesus's sacrifice on the cross, or maybe they weren't. Their lives, however, did prove they had made Jesus both Savior and Lord of their lives. And while the text is not perfectly clear, it appears as if the believers at Ephesus were saved and baptized to receive salvation all at once.

The particulars are not what matters. The important fact is whether one has made Jesus Christ their Savior through faith and their Lord by declaration and obedience to His Word. Following with water baptism is a matter of obedience and an outward display and celebration of what has happened within one's heart.

So, if someone has no desire to be baptized, perhaps their salvation has not yet occurred. As I said earlier, we have enough of scripture available to us so that we understand the way to the Father through His Son Jesus Christ.

Have you been baptized since you believed?

# Day 180

## Wisdom in Relationships

2 Kings 15-16 / Acts 19:13-41 / Psalm 147 / Proverbs 18:4-5

Wisdom is not something I've claimed in the past to possess, but just as the Lord has allowed me to hear His voice and now to see in the Spirit, He wants me to walk in the wisdom I have. It is no longer true that I don't have wisdom, so I'm no longer permitted to say that.

When I get stuck on what to do, I pray and ask God for wisdom. I also ask my hubby Jeff because he is one who is peaceful and wise. He has a way of building bridges with others and of diffusing situations that would otherwise be blown completely out of proportion.

Jeff is a residential contractor, so he's had more than twenty years of dealing with customers and homeowners who were in varying degrees of satisfaction on how their jobs were progressing. He's had people angry at him and cursing him. He's been fired from jobs for various reasons, most of which were misunderstandings. What does Jeff do when someone is angry or cursing? He remains calm and usually brings the conversation back to reason.

But he's also not afraid to let these people know that he won't be talked to that way. And we should also have the right to speak up for ourselves or remove ourselves from situations that are out of control.

Wisdom will look different in each situation. At times, we should speak up and at times we should walk away. Sometimes it's hard to know when to respond and how.

Proverbs 18:4 tell us,

"Wise words are like deep waters;
wisdom flows from the wise like a bubbling brook."

"Wisdom," "deep waters," "a bubbling brook." Reading these words gives us a peaceful picture. I am remembering another scripture regarding God's wisdom.

"But the wisdom from above is first of all pure.
It is also peace loving, gentle at all times,
and willing to yield to others. It is full of mercy
and the fruit of good deeds. It shows no favoritism
and is always sincere."
— James 3:17

I think I want wisdom to be my best friend! And as a follower of Christ, that's possible because wisdom is not just a concept. It is the person of Jesus Christ. Reading these descriptions gives us peace and brings us to conviction because we must ask ourselves if we operate this way when relating with others.

I recently had to work through a misunderstanding with a friend I've known for many years. She was upset over something she thought I did, which I didn't do. And the accusations made me upset because I had hoped she knew me better. She wanted to walk away, and frankly, so did I. But God wouldn't allow that. So, after I calmed down, forgave her, and prayed, I set up a coffee date.

The good news is all is well between us. The enemy was attempting to get in there and ruin what we had worked so hard to repair and rebuild. He lost the battle this time!

Let's go down the list of what wisdom is according to these verses in James. Wisdom is pure, peace-loving, gentle, willing to yield (humble, reasonable), full of mercy, full of good deeds, unwavering and sincere.

Let's look these words up in the Strong's Concordance to see if we can gain anything further.

"Pure" is defined as "pure from carnality and every fault, innocent."

"Peace-loving" is defined "brings peace with it."

"Gentle" is "appropriate, patient."

"Reasonable" is "compliant, obeys easily."

"Full of mercy" is "kindness or good will towards the miserable and the afflicted, joined with a desire to help them."

"Full of good fruits" is "joyful, happy, excellent, honorable works."

"Unwavering" is "impartial (shows no favoritism.)"

"Without hypocrisy" and "sincere" is "undisguised, with no mask on."

I appreciate the broadening of understanding these definitions bring. With my friend, I needed to choose all of these, and it wasn't easy at first, but as I prayed, I knew God would give me the words when in the moment. He did. I found myself being honest and keeping to the boundaries I needed, but also gentle, merciful, sincere and as the original verse stated, willing to yield.

Although I had done nothing wrong, my friend was rattled at

something she thought I had done, and her heart was shaken. She told me with tears in her eyes that this pain reminded her of past pains, and I understood that all too well. I'm thankful I did the hard thing and didn't allow the enemy to rob us of our friendship, our peace and yes, our wisdom.

# Day 181

## The Gift of Grace

2 Kings 17:1-18:12 / Acts 20 / Psalm 148 / Proverbs 18:6-7

Does any of you ever feel that Christianity is too difficult to follow? Or that there are too many rules to remember? Since Christianity has in its history the practices of the people of Israel with the 10 commandments, and the additional 600+ rules the Pharisees instituted, some believe we must try to keep up with all the previous regulations. That, however, is not true. Christianity is simple when looked at through the lens of what Jesus Christ accomplished!

That's a relief to me, because all my life I've tried to be a good person not fully realizing what Jesus's sacrifice purchased for me. Jesus's sacrifice and my acceptance of Him does not mean I can live any way I'd like either! Instead, I'm free to live a life of grace and love through the forgiveness He offered. I say "offered" because we must receive that offer for it to become ours.

Think of it this way. You received a coupon in the mail for a discount when you purchase a certain item. However, unless you put in the coupon code or take the coupon with you to the store, you won't receive the discount. You must redeem the coupon.

Let's compare that to salvation. Just because Jesus has paid the price and made the offer, we must still receive the gift before it's ours. I'm thinking of all this based on Acts 20:32 which states,

"And now I entrust you to God and the message of His grace
that is able to build you up and give you an inheritance
with all those He has set apart for himself."

The portion of that I'm interested in looking at further is "grace that is able to build you up and give you an inheritance." Grace builds me up and grace gives me an inheritance.

Did you notice it doesn't say, "The Law builds me up and gives me an inheritance"? Nor does it state that keeping the law will give me these things. I can't be good enough to earn any of what Jesus has paid for and offered; I must receive all He did through faith by His grace.

Our next question might be, "What is Grace?" Once I understand grace, how does it build me up? How does grace give me an inheritance? Let's study and find out!

"Grace" is the Greek word "charis," which means "of the merciful kindness by which God, exerting his holy influence upon souls, turns them to Christ, keeps, strengthens, increases them in Christian faith, knowledge, affection, and kindles them to the exercise of the Christian virtues."

"To build you up" is the Greek word "epoikodomeo," which means "in the N. T. only in the figurative which likens a company of Christian believers to an edifice or temple; to build upon, build up; absolute – 'to finish the structure of which the foundation has already been laid,' i. e. in plain language, to give constant increase in Christian knowledge and in a life conformed thereto."

"To give you an inheritance" is the Greek word

"kleronomia," which is "property to be received (aka the Kingdom of God.)"

So, if I receive the message of His grace, I have everything I will ever need. I need nothing more. Grace is enough. Jesus Christ and what He accomplished on the cross is enough. I can't earn more even if I try. I'll just wear myself out trying to be more approved when I'm already as approved by God as I'll ever be once I'm in Christ.

And, if you read the definition of "grace" again, you'll see that by us sharing this message, everyone around us will also have everything they need. We won't have to prop them up, because they will be empowered by God's grace to accomplish all He's given them to do.

I have one last thought. The very end of that verse tells us that our inheritance is found with all those He has set apart. In other words, I cannot receive this grace in a vacuum or all by myself. This grace is received as I commit to community with other followers of Jesus Christ. If you want the goods, you gotta love the people!

# Day 182

## The Lord is our Defender

2 Kings 18:13-19:37 / Acts 21:1-17 / Psalm 149 / Proverbs 18:8

All of us have had people speak evil of us, threaten us, or just plain say rude and untrue things. We have several options when this happens. We can get angry and speak evil words back at that person. We can try to reason with them, showing them why they are wrong to speak that way. Or we can ignore them, knowing that what God says about us is what carries weight.

The story of King Hezekiah, a godly king in 2 Kings, is indicative of attacks we all experience. Just because we are in Christ, just because we belong to the Lord, that does not mean we won't suffer attacks. Evil still exists and the enemy is always attempting to devise a way to derail our lives with his horrible plans.

I love that Hezekiah stood strong in the face of the king of Assyria and his leaders as they threatened to attack and destroy the city of Judah. They taunted, they mocked Israel's God, and they promised suffering, but in the end, the Lord upheld His own glory and His own Name. And He will also do that for us!

Hezekiah would not respond to the verbal threats, nor would he allow his people to respond. They were told to ignore the words being hurled at them. Then Hezekiah asked the Lord for help, both through the prophet Isaiah and by going himself into the temple and laying the threats before God's presence. And God answered!

Not only did Hezekiah not have to fight, nor did his people suffer any harm, but the angel of the Lord also wiped out 185,000 of the enemy as they slept. All Judah had to do was pray and ask for God's help, and God answered by defending His people.

"For my own honor and for the sake of my servant David,
I will defend this city and protect it."
—1 Kings 19:34,

Another truth we need to keep in mind is that the Lord guards
His own Word and His own honor. We do not have to guard God's
honor; He's quite capable of that all on His own. I also do not believe
we have to guard our honor because God also promises to defend us.

"Dear friends, never take revenge.
Leave that to the righteous anger of God.
For the Scriptures say, 'I will take revenge.
I will pay them back,' says the Lord."
— Romans 12:19

Never take revenge. Never. Can you commit to doing that?
Several years ago, after Jeff and I were falsely accused and treated hor-
ribly, the Lord reminded us of this verse and told us not to respond
to those who were persecuting us unjustly. That was hard because we
wanted to defend ourselves, but we realized that it was much better
to allow God to defend us because He is always just.

So, the next time someone goads and taunts you, turn away
and pray, asking God to defend you. Listen to how He wants you to
respond, then obey. Then, watch to see what He does.

It may take a while for the results of the taunting to fall on
those who are persecuting you, but it will be much better for you
if you do not engage. You will have peace of mind, and you'll be
able to rejoice when you see the Lord defend you!

# Biography

Maria Kear began her Jesus journey when she received Christ at the age of five. That dramatic encounter with Him set her up for a life filled with a spiritual hunger that compels her to not only seek after God wholeheartedly, but also to create hunger and thirst in others through her words, experience and life example.

Maria and her husband Jeff have three adult children and as of this writing they have four grandchildren with more promised in the future.

Maria and Jeff launched a house church called Bethesda Springs House of Mercy and Grace in July 2020 when the Lord surprised them with His plans as they fasted and prayed just prior.

Maria has many fond sayings, one of which is, "I want to leave this earth with my hair still on fire!"

May your "hair" catch fire as you read and become hungrier for Him.